Eyes Online: Eyes On Life is ... he ... ... ntroduced
to that exposes destructive ... ... are... ...
powerful, with real life a... ... ...porn ...raphy
and other obsessive behaviors, and recovery was hard.
As I read this book, I wished Jan Kern had written it four or five
years earlier so it could have helped me at the time of my struggle. For
the person who struggles with obsessive online behaviors, this book,
along with God's help, will take him or her on a powerful journey to
recovery.

— Mike Bowling, aspiring journalist

As those created in God's image, we're made to live in a real world.
For one reason or another many teens find themselves spending a
great deal of their time and energy living a virtual existence—one that
disconnects them from their true design and potential. This book can
help awaken teens from the disembodied experience of online life to
the fulfillment and joy God intends for them to know.

—Olivia and Kurt Bruner, authors of *Playstation Nation:
Protect Your Child from Video Game Addiction*

This book really hit home for me. My problems and my addiction don't
seem so uncommon. The feelings of loneliness and not being wanted
are not reserved only for me. I see hope. I see a way of change through
the interactions and help of others, and more importantly, through
God. Now I realize I don't have to be ruled by my addiction or struggle
on my own. *Eyes Online : Eyes On Life* has given me hope that I can
overcome, that I can do all things through Christ.

—Dean Byrd, student

Jan Kern writes with insight, passion, and wisdom as she chronicles the struggles of young people who have become caught in compulsive Internet use. Her counsel to teens—or anyone else dealing with online obsessive behavior—is grounded in sound Christian principles and benefits from the insights of leading experts in the emerging field of Internet addiction. Teens, parents, and youth pastors everywhere should read this book.

— Andrew Careaga, author, *Hooked on the Net* and *eMinistry: Connecting with the Net Generation*

Eyes Online : Eyes on Life gripped me by the throat and wouldn't let go. This powerful, compelling story brought me face to face with the Internet struggles of my generation. Armed with practical helps and suggestions, this book helps me feel equipped to come alongside those who are desperately searching for help.

—B.J. Hamrick, freelance journalist

Timely, eye-opening, and extremely practical, *Eyes Online : Eyes On Life* draws out the serious seduction that many kids, especially guys, experience through Internet activities. Every teen or young adult should read Jan Kern's book and pass it on to his or her parents.

—Meg Meeker, physician, author of *Boys Should Be Boys* and *Restoring the Teenage Soul*

Internet obsession is one of many ways that individuals try to fill the void or emptiness caused by a lack of connection to family, friends, and especially God. Jan has done an excellent job capturing the words of Colin and others as they go through the process of becoming disenchanted with their lives and becoming detached from God, their friends, and family. *Eyes Online : Eyes On Life* is a continuation of a series of excellent books that provide a road map for the individual, concerned friend, or family member through the process of recovery. As the author states, it is a courageous journey. I, too, pray that readers take it.

—Thom A. P. Smith, EdD, marriage and family therapist

This was an awesome read. It's tough to find books that challenge you to do better, and I love that about this book. Like a lot of Christian teens, I'd never stopped to consider that maybe I wasn't honoring God with my Internet use. Reading Jan's *Eyes Online : Eyes on Life* has challenged me to view the way I spend my time online through God's eyes. This isn't just a story about Internet addicts—it's a story of redeeming love and what can happen when we let God in.

—Debra Weiss, high school student

EYES ONLINE : EYES ON LIFE

A JOURNEY OUT OF ONLINE ADDICTIONS // **JAN KERN**

A LIVE FREE BOOK

EYES ONLINE : EYES ON LIFE

Standard®
PUBLISHING
Bringing The Word to Life

Cincinnati, Ohio

Published by Standard Publishing, Cincinnati, Ohio
www.standardpub.com

Printed in the United States of America

Project editor: Robert Irvin
Cover design: Studio Gearbox
Interior design: Edward Willis Group, Inc.

All Scripture quotations, unless otherwise indicated, are taken from the Holy Bible, NEW INTERNATIONAL VERSION®. NIV®. Copyright © 1973, 1978, 1984 by International Bible Society. Used by permission of Zondervan. All rights reserved. Scripture quotations marked *NLT* are taken from the Holy Bible, *New Living Translation.* Copyright © 1996, 2004. Used by permission of Tyndale House Publishers, Inc., Wheaton, Illinois 60189. All rights reserved. Scripture quotations marked *The Message* are taken from *The Message.* Copyright © 1993, 1994, 1995, 1996, 2000, 2001, 2002, by NavPress Publishing Group. Used by permission. All rights reserved.

Published in association with the Books & Such Literary Agency, 52 Mission Circle, Suite 122, PMB 170, Santa Rosa, CA 95409-5370, www.booksandsuch.biz.

ISBN 978-0-7847-2159-9

Library of Congress Cataloging-in-Publication Data

Kern, Jan, 1956-
  Eyes online, eyes on life : a journey out of online addictions / Jan Kern.
    p. cm.
 "A Live Free book."
  ISBN 978-0-7847-2159-9 (perfect bound)
  1. Christian teenagers--Religious life. 2. Internet addicts--Religious life. 3. Internet addiction--Religious aspects--Christianity. I. Title.

BV4531.3.K46 2008
241'.667--dc22

                                                                    2008017611

14 13 12 11 10 09 08   9 8 7 6 5 4 3 2 1

DEDICATION

To my family—Tom, Sarah, Danny, Marci, and "The Ranch" community: Your love, support, and expressions of Christ's servant nature always keep me pushing forward. You are amazing.

CONTENTS

I CAN QUIT ANYTIME I WANT TO . . .

Hi, my name is Tom, and I'm an addict.

I don't have a problem with the bottle or with any kind of pharmaceutical product, legal or illegal. No, my problem is with games. I'm addicted to them.

When in high school I was obsessed with bowling to the point where, if I saw a group of people standing around, I automatically calculated where I'd need to aim the bowling ball in order to knock them all over. I was a pinball junkie, and then there were Pac-Man, Centipede, and Galaxian. Many a quarter vanished into those games as I sought a quick fix. I then discovered computer solitaire, and I came to rue the day I put that first red "2" over a black ace.

And now the Internet has made this potential to get hooked all too easy. My particular poison these days is online Scrabble. I play a game every day upon getting home from work, and if for some reason I can't I feel a bit agitated. In a previous generation I'd be the dad who comes home from work and pours himself a stiff drink. (I'm glad that looking for the ultimate triple-word score carries fewer potential problems than does alcohol!)

But this raises an important point: A lot of people think the only potential problem with going online is the content of the Web sites themselves. Pornography. Violence. Language.

Sure, we have to be careful about those things, but that isn't a problem in Scrabble. The problem is in the *process*. Hours spent staring into a computer screen reading friends' Facebook pages are hours that are gone forever. So are hours spent on a role-playing game such as World of Warcraft—or Scrabble, for that matter. The very process of going to even "safe" sites may be setting you up for future problems.

Jan Kern has chosen an apt title for this book—*Eyes Online : Eyes on Life*. For increasing numbers of young people, real life is losing out to online life. Whether it's an obsession with online social sites such as Facebook or MySpace, MMORPGs (massively multiplayer online role-playing games) or pornography—often all at the same time—young people find themselves unable to tear away from the computer screen to experience real life. As a result, sports, hobbies, and schoolwork usually suffer.

As with any addiction, the solution first lies in getting the person to admit he or she has a problem. That's what happened in my case. I came to realize that my Scrabble obsession was affecting my home life. So while I still enjoy the game, I'm careful to limit my time staring at the screen.

As you read this book, you'll see that Jan is forthright in discussing the problem, and many readers might recognize themselves in its pages. But Jan shows great compassion for those caught up in one of the newest forms of addiction.

More important, she offers hope and a way out and points readers to the source of that hope: faith in Jesus Christ.

If you know someone who's caught in the snare of Internet addiction, give him or her this book. It might be the first step in breaking free.

—Tom Neven, editorial director,
Focus on the Family Youth Outreach

FACING REALITY . . .

THE INTERNET—it can offer a really great experience, or for some, it can easily become an obsession. Without realizing it, we're sucked into activities that rob us of the amazing identity, resources, and relationships God has in mind for us.

When Colin first got online, he was ten years old. It didn't take long for him to discover a whole new world on the Internet . . . and to fall into its traps. Not everyone gets caught in those. But not everyone who gets caught realizes it, either.

Colin has an honest story to tell, an honest perspective. Being connected online is still part of his daily world, but not in the same way it used to be. He's not afraid to admit where his Internet use took him or the depths of the battles he fought. It takes courage to look at the reality of anything we do that might be harmful and be open about how it impacts us on the different levels of who we are. Colin has that courage.

You might recognize a bit of yourself in his story or the stories of others included in this book. If something about their stories stirs you and challenges you to a different, better place, be assured that God will give you the courage to go there, just as he did for Colin.

Maybe you know someone who needs a closer look into his or her online activities. Use this book—there are lots of suggestion boxes along the way—to consider ways to support and encourage, then walk alongside your friend or family member through the struggles. Offer accountability and mentoring. Colin and others have found that kind of support, and it helped.

Colin's story is very real, so many of the names in the story are also real. In some instances, names have been changed when people have not been available to share their perspective or to give consent to the use of their names. The name of one of Colin's older brothers is included in the book, but another older brother chose to remain unnamed. Also, for privacy, most of the names of those who offered their perspectives and stories in the commentary have been changed.

Names changed.

That happens often online. Roles are played. Identities are masked. The Internet is a huge part of our lives, but I hope you won't ever feel you have to hide your identity when it comes to being honest with God about your online activities. He cares deeply about you—the real you with all your hurts, struggles, and longings.

A prayer you can pray:

> *God, being online is a part of my daily life. It's really easy to spend time there and get caught up in activities that keep me from being all you created me to be, from doing all that you created me to do. It's especially easy to slide into believing what I do on the Internet doesn't matter so much. Give me the courage to consider where you are leading me about my online choices, and give me the strength to go there. Amen.*

Praying for your courageous journey,

one

I felt like the Internet was where I belonged.

COLIN LEANED FORWARD IN HIS CHAIR. The soft creak didn't register, but then neither did the songs playing through his iPod. The images and words on the computer monitor drew his full attention.

Another shooting at a school, this time on a college campus.

Though far away, this one was more devastating than others he'd heard about. He shook his head, studied the monitor. *How did it happen?*

Colin clicked and followed links to site after site and took in more details of the story. Finally, he drew in a breath and sat back in his chair. Still staring at the screen, he slid his desk drawer open and popped out a quirky ball that fit in the palm of his hand. Colin's hands were never still for long. As he pounded the ball from one palm to the other, a red light pulsed from the center of the open, twisted bands of rubber.

> **More questions pulsed through his mind.**
> **Emotions flashed. Anger one moment,**
> **sadness the next. Tears burned.**
> **He coughed and swallowed.**

What set the guy off? Didn't anyone see this coming? Could it have been prevented?

More questions pulsed through his mind. Emotions flashed. Anger one moment, sadness the next. Tears burned. He coughed and swallowed.

Colin dropped the ball back into the drawer. A final red blink flickered as he slid the drawer shut. He set an elbow on the desk, leaned his chin into his hand, and with the other hand clicked on a new link.

Some of the victims had run and hidden. Some played dead. The stories were conflicted on details like how many were shot and how many had died, but there were a lot. Even from miles away, it seemed starkly real—not like some video game that people can walk away from.

Colin shuddered. He reached up, pushed his glasses up his nose, and adjusted one of his earphones. As the final notes of a Relient K song faded into a Switchfoot mix, he dropped his hand back to the mouse. He tapped his fingers. He wanted to do something, make a difference . . . But how?

> **Colin felt the anger rise again.**
> *Man, how could he do it?*
> **He shook his head and sat back.**

In the quietness of the pause between songs, voices buzzed from another room, shifting his attention. He pulled off his earphones, and the wires dropped around his neck. He heard the phone ring, someone answering. He picked up a pen from his desk and twirled it over his thumb and through his fingers. As he did, he nodded his head along with the beat of a drumming rhythm he made with his tongue. The sounds around him grew quiet. He looked back at the screen.

What had he been doing? *Oh yeah, the story . . .*

Maybe he'd create a tribute to the victims. A video scenario ran through his mind. He imagined designing the video, accompanying it with a song he'd play on the piano and sing.

He tossed the pen onto his desk and reread the story on the monitor. A couple more clicks and a link showed a picture of the alleged shooter's face. Colin felt the anger rise again. *Man, how could he do it?* He shook his head and sat back. The eyes of the shooter seemed to stare into his. Then it hit him. The injured and killed weren't the only victims. The guy who shot them was a victim too. A person. Someone he could have known.

Colin swallowed. Could he ever have gotten so desperate, angry, or hurting to do what this guy did—go off and shoot people? Colin shook his head in answer to his own question. But . . . he sure could understand him in a lot of ways. If he were there, walking the hallways with the guy, seeing him on the streets, he would have recognized the signs—the confusion and fear in his eyes, the raw loneliness . . .

Those thoughts sucked him back to a time—not too distant—of his own loneliness. He had felt it for years, like a menacing shadow he couldn't shake. The taunting when he was younger, the uncomfortable feelings of being left out, some of it by his own choice. The kids in elementary school talking about something sexual or getting a cheap thrill by being disrespectful to teachers or bullying other kids. He hadn't wanted to be part of it. Sometimes he only was because he happened to be the one they were targeting.

Then in junior high, he'd joined in on some of it just to fit in. Or at least to be left alone. The loneliness still followed him from one year to the next, right into high school. He had felt it everywhere—at church, sometimes even at home. But school, that was the worst. He showed up every day and would rather have been anywhere else. Sure, at lunch he hung out with a few friends he knew from band, sometimes laughing and cracking jokes. Mostly he just got through those days, avoiding as much interaction as possible.

> **Just as a bell rang for class, he felt an arm come across his shoulder. Two guys closed in and flanked him while he walked. Big guys.**

Still, there was Lisa. She was nice. They were friends, hanging out during band period and band events. They talked. Sometimes, as friends, held hands or hugged. Then one day, even that friendship was threatened, and he became the target of bullying again. He remembered it well. He was walking between some buildings on campus. The sun's heat pierced his T-shirt. Just as a bell rang for class, he felt an arm come across his shoulder. Two guys closed in and flanked him while he walked. Big guys—bigger than he was, anyway. One—Matt— he'd known from earth science class.

"You've been hanging out a lot with Lisa," Matt had said. The other guy, whose arm squeezed down on him, added, "Yeah,

I don't want to see you hanging around my girlfriend anymore." Colin had pegged these guys as mostly talk, but still able to inflict damage if they wanted. Their purpose was to intimidate, and they had accomplished it big time. As they walked away, his heart beat hard in his chest. He remembered the sickening dread that spread like thick goo in his stomach. It stayed with him through the last couple of class periods of that day.

> **He sat there, legs stretched, one foot tapping. His heartbeat had calmed, but he couldn't shake the feeling that stuck in his stomach.**

When he got home, he'd skipped his usual routine of grabbing something to eat or drink. He headed straight for his room, dropped his stuff on his bed, and slid into his chair in front of the computer. He sat there, legs stretched, one foot tapping. His heartbeat had calmed, but he couldn't shake the feeling that stuck in his stomach. He scooted his chair toward the monitor and jumped online.

The great escape. That day after school, he knew it would work.

Colin picked up the pen again, tapping it on his knee as his thoughts slid back to the college shooter's face. Maybe that guy had tried to escape too—from fears, loneliness, something. He only needed one good friend. Just one. Someone to tell him he mattered. Someone to listen.

Maybe I could have been that friend.

The video tribute still formed in Colin's thoughts and played through his mind. *Someone to listen.* Would the guy have been willing to talk about what was going on inside? Could lives have been saved? Maybe. Maybe not.

Loneliness. Not a good thing. Not a good thing at all.

Again Colin's thoughts took him back to the day Matt and Lisa's boyfriend had threatened him.

> **Lisa was one of the few good things about school. When they were talking and laughing together, he could forget how lonely other times of the day or week were.**
>
> http://

It had felt natural to turn to the Internet to shake what happened. It was where he spent most of his time—especially by the time he was in high school. . . .

Even in the afternoon his bedroom remained mostly dark, except for the glow from the monitor. Lights were off. The blinds were drawn closed. As Colin sat at his computer, he could almost feel the guy's arm across his shoulder, still pressing down. Leave his girlfriend alone? He didn't even know Lisa *had* a boyfriend—at least not one that serious.

Lisa was one of the few good things about school. When they were talking and laughing together, he could forget how lonely other times of the day or week were.

That day his online activities started out simple, innocent. He opened his e-mail, checked his inbox, read a couple of messages. He clicked on video game bulletin boards and joined a chat about codes and the latest hot video games. While he read those, he IM'd several friends he'd gotten to know online. Maybe he'd tell one of them what happened that day.

The afternoon hours pushed toward dinnertime as he moved away from chatting and got involved in a game of RuneScape. His avatar teleporting across the realm of Gielinor reflected in his glasses. Eyes and mind completely focused, he maneuvered through the fantasy kingdoms, fighting monsters and completing quests. With the background sounds of music and seagulls screeching, he was pulled into a world far away from the guys who'd threatened him, far from the uncomfortable realm of the high school halls and passageways.

Food smells coming from the kitchen made his stomach growl. He ignored it.

"Come eat some dinner," his dad said as he passed Colin's room.

"OK, Dad," he grumbled. Colin shifted and clicked his mouse a few more times to fight off a monster; he got to a safe part of an island and closed the game. He pushed away from his computer. As he stepped into the hallway and then the lighted living room, he blinked a few times to adjust to the brightness. Dad was sitting in front of the TV, already eating.

"I made spaghetti and a salad," Mom said. She was standing at the kitchen counter blending a meal shake for Chris, Colin's older brother, who had mental retardation. Mealtimes were a challenge for Mom, so they often ate wherever, instead of at the dining room table.

"Thanks, Mom. I'll just have a hot dog."

"OK. There's plenty if you change your mind."

"Yeah, I know. Thanks for making dinner. I'm just not that hungry." He kept his choices to a few favorites. He knew she wouldn't press the issue.

> His thoughts about the day grew more distant, as if he were walling them up in some forgotten corridor. Not a place he planned to return to—if possible, not ever.

Colin warmed his hot dog and bun in the microwave, wrapped it in a paper towel, and headed back to his room. He didn't want to watch TV tonight. The day's events too easily pushed into his mind again and got him down. He'd avoid that any way he could. He bit into his hot dog as he settled back into his desk chair.

Outside it had grown darker. The monitor's soft light cast a glow across his room. Colin took a few more bites and used his free hand to check e-mail and message boards again. As he popped in the last bite, he wiped his hand on his jeans and opened RuneScape to resume his game. His thoughts about the day grew more distant, as if he were walling them up in some forgotten corridor. Not a place he planned to return to—if possible, not ever.

A couple of hours passed quickly. Sounds coming from the other rooms and passing down the hall told Colin that Chris, then Mom and Dad, were heading to bed. Mom and Dad poked their heads in at different times to say good-night.

"Don't stay up too late, Colin," Mom said.

"Yeah, OK." Colin nodded a good-night.

After a little more time passed, Colin checked the quietness of the house. He was sure everyone was asleep by now, but he listened again. Hearing nothing, he turned to other Internet activities he felt might ease the unrest of the day and his loneliness.

A few clicks and . . . he was trapped. No internal alarms went off to warn him of what was coming. The seduction over time had been gradual—jaws clamping down, deceptive, drawing Colin in deeper and deeper.

> As I sink in despair, my spirit ebbing away,
> you know how I'm feeling,
> know the danger I'm in,
> the traps hidden in my path.
>
> PSALM 142:3 (*THE MESSAGE*)

A PLACE WITHOUT EXPECTATIONS

The Internet. It was where Colin felt he belonged.

From his early years in school, he had picked up the clear message from others that he was different. He didn't fit in the way they expected. Later, he struggled with feeling uncomfortable in any social situation. "I had decided it wasn't OK for me to be social," he recalled later.

Colin had no huge aspirations to be popular. He looked enough like his peers in his jeans and T-shirts, but generally he shrugged it off if they thought he didn't have the right look or the right friends. Still, he felt the pressure and grew weary of the bullying. The Internet became the one place the expectations and taunting wouldn't press in on him. He could be himself—or anyone he wanted to be. "All those people online never judged me on my appearance," he said. "They never saw me. But the people at school saw me daily, and they had me judged before they even knew me."

In the early years of his Internet use, Colin's online time was monitored and limited by his mom and dad. He wasn't getting into any trouble with it, so as time passed, they checked up on his activities less and less. By ninth grade, when he had his own computer in his room, time online naturally increased. He remembered, "Anytime I was at home, I'd go on the Internet. I'd be there for hours at a time."

For many, an hour or more online—or even a few hours—isn't a problem. For Colin, one thing led to another. The Internet became the world he preferred. He didn't recognize it at the time, but when he looked back he saw it clearly: "I was so trapped in the Internet world, no person could possibly drag me out."

> Be a patient friend to someone who seems quieter and on the fringes of the group you're involved in. Invite him to join in, but be understanding if he isn't ready. Talk to him about the activities he likes. Keep an open discussion about computer use if that's one of his interests.

You click online and you've just connected to something that has a sense of infinity. No way in a lifetime could you see everything, do everything, talk to everyone. There's always more. It's exciting, stimulating, or just so much a part of your daily world that it's a natural place to spend your time. Online you chat with friends, connect with groups that have similar interests, check e-mail, play games, look up information, shop, and find lots more ways to express your creativity and interests.

The Internet is here to stay, and in the next ten or twenty years it'll likely grow in its capabilities in ways we can't even imagine.

But people like Colin and others have found that, along with all the amazing innovation and positive experiences they've found there, being online also has been a downfall for them—big time. When they're being really honest, they talk about the lines they've crossed. Sometimes without even realizing it, they've been consumed by being online with simple activities like chatting, checking e-mail, blogging, or posting and commenting on blogs. Some have discovered games or activities they can't stop thinking about even when they finally walk away from the computer. Others have ventured onto X-rated sites and found themselves lured by sexual traps that turned into secret addictions.

At fifteen, Mark was often online until three or four in the morning. He spent most of that time just doing normal stuff—looking up information he was interested in, chatting, or reading blogs. Eventually he had a list of thirty blogs that he regularly read and commented on. Keeping up with that ate up his time. But Mark also found another interest that became consuming. He began to visit a site where he would read sex-related fiction. "I found some of the dark corners of the Internet," he said.

Melissa got into blogging on a popular journaling site. She found herself returning to the site often to network with others. The line she believes she crossed? "I started writing out my thoughts compulsively every day." Now she warns, "All things in moderation, and the moment you feel slightly out of control, you're probably a lot more out of control than you realize, or want to admit."

Today, you'll also find Melissa playing one of her favorite online role-playing games, World of Warcraft (WoW). She says it's fun, and she enjoys the social interaction and creating end goals. But she adds, "It's really easy to make those goals your focus and ignore your life goals." She feels everyone who plays has to admit they've slipped into doing that at least once.

Mike shared what he feels is crossing the line: "Being online and doing things online isn't bad in itself, but you need to make sure you've got a good grasp on keeping time limits on yourself and making sure that what you're doing and how much of what you're doing is healthy."

This book is about what you're doing online. It's also about what's happening in your life that takes you to those moments where destructive choices are made and lines are crossed. And if you've found yourself in one of those moments, it's about where you go from here.

You don't have to be an expert on computers or the Internet to be a great support person for someone who struggles with online activity. Still, be willing to learn some basic information about the current trends and what teens are into. Do some online research or ask a young adult who's willing to fill you in.

A WARNING METER

You're moving through your day, and suddenly you hear a warning beep so shrill you have to cover your ears. You look down toward your chest, about where your heart is, and you see a meter. It's flashing. You're losing life energy fast, and the decisions you make in the next few moments are crucial. What are you going to do to restore that energy? The next move you make has to be the right one or . . . you die. Game over.

OK, maybe not.

We don't have flashing, beeping meters hanging outside our bodies to warn us of anything. God didn't make us that way. But he did create us with a heart and a conscience that can pretty effectively warn us of dangers and traps we might be walking into—if we stay sensitive and willing to consider his leading.

Jesus said, "Blessed are the poor in spirit, for theirs is the kingdom of heaven" (Matthew 5:3).

Poor in spirit. That condition of the spirit is, in a way, one of our internal warning meters. "But," we might say, "it almost sounds like something is weak or broken." So are we in trouble?

Only if we totally miss that *poor* really *is* the condition of our own spirits. And that it's OK to understand we're in that condition.

Every person has an impoverished spirit, one that's ragged, lacking, and in need of God. But when Jesus said, "Blessed are the poor in spirit," he meant that you're in a great place when you're living in a way that recognizes that condition. It can be hard to see yourself that way, but there's something good about it. It's in moments when you fully accept the stark reality of your spiritual need that you clearly see God's love for you and welcome his help in every area of your life.

When we take that truth beyond just a moment of awareness to actually being a part of how we live out each day, we're more likely to bring God along when we go online. He'll help us make choices, and we won't fall for the traps.

God, you see me as an individual, and you love me. You know all my struggles, my hurts, and my weaknesses. And you know the traps I can easily fall into. Help me see and accept the full reality of my spiritual condition and my need for you. Then help me accept your participation in all areas of my life, including what I choose to do with my time online. AMEN.

So if the Son sets you free, you are truly free.
JOHN 8:36 (*NLT*)

GOING DEEPER

■ Take a moment to list all of your favorite online activities. Which ones have the potential to become traps for you personally?

■ Sometimes we aren't aware that what we're doing is consuming our time or thoughts. For a day or week, track how much time you spend on each of your online activities. Are there any that could be slipping toward being, as Melissa found, out of control?

■ While you're online how well are you listening to your internal warning meter? Read John 16:8 and think about how the Spirit works to make us aware of things. What areas of spiritual growth can you bring to God to ask for his help? For instance, hearing God, seeking him for direction, including him more in daily decisions and activities, praying or reading the Bible more.

DEEPER STILL

Take a walk, go for a run, pray and think, or just talk with someone. Whatever you choose, spend some time considering your relationship with God. Ask him to help you see yourself as he does—greatly loved by him, but also very much in need of him.

After you've taken a closer look, spend a few moments writing down what he showed you. Finish by writing a prayer of thanks.

two

The more I used the Internet,
the more I had the opportunity and the harder it was to resist.
More chances to check out other stuff. More clicks.

TEN-YEAR-OLD COLIN SQUIRMED IN HIS CHAIR as he watched his dad slide the mouse and click to connect to the Internet.

"OK, once we're online I'll get you going with your new e-mail address."

Colin nodded in response and sat back while he listened to the audible dial of the phone and then the screech of the computer's modem. He swung one leg back and forth and wished it didn't take so long. The sound finally stopped and a box popped up on the screen, ticking the seconds and showing the connection speed.

Dad clicked open the e-mail program. Colin sat forward again. He kept his expression casual even with the excitement he felt buzzing inside. He was getting his own e-mail address. Until then he really hadn't used the computer much. He liked his video games, and that kept him plenty busy.

"I've already set up your account, so here's where you'll check if you have any messages." Dad pointed and clicked on the inbox. "Then when you want to send a message to someone, you just ..."

Colin watched the arrow move across the screen; he took in every word and instruction. He fidgeted in his chair, ready to try it himself.

"So there you go. Want to give it a shot?"

"Sure." Colin scooted forward.

"Let me know if you have any questions." Dad stood and stepped away.

With the family computer set up in one corner of the kitchen, Colin heard every move his dad made, including when he opened the refrigerator door and began scrounging through the shelves for something to eat.

Colin's fingers tapped the edge of the keyboard while he thought about what he could do. Not much. The only e-mail address he knew was his dad's. He opened a new message window and pecked out:

```
hi Dad.
thanks for setting up my e-mail
Colin
```

He clicked to send his message and waited for the confirmation that it had been sent. The box popped up and he closed it.

He sat staring at the monitor. Now what? He shrugged, disconnected from the Internet, got up, and went next door to Lissa's house to play.

Colin slid into the chair in front of the computer and let out a long sigh. Not a good day at school at all. Sixth grade was no better than fifth—he was *still* ignored and teased. Several months had passed. He'd quickly grown more comfortable with the Internet. He decided he liked messing around online. He could always find something to do, someone new to talk to.

In those months since he'd started using the Internet, he'd found new friends in a chat room.

"Watch your time," his dad said as he passed by.

"OK, Dad."

He connected and signed into the chat room, where he hoped to meet some of those he'd found online before. Usually they talked about school, about video games they played, just stuff. He was glad he could relax with them. They weren't like the kids at school who judged him before he even had a chance to show who he was.

> **He could always find something to do, someone new to talk to. In those months since he'd started using the Internet, he'd found new friends in a chat room.**

He sighed. It felt good to have conversations with people who seemed to like talking to him, even if he'd probably never meet them in real life.

The chat window opened, and Colin saw that a few he knew were already there. *Cool.* He joined in. While he waited for a response to a comment, he glanced around the kitchen. Mom was in and out, busy with Chris. Dad had just come home from work. Colin looked back toward the screen. He'd try to keep the chat conversation going and stay on as long as his parents would let him.

People signed in and out of the chat room. In between comments, Colin clicked around, looking up information on video games. Mom came into the kitchen and dug her keys out of an empty brown coffee can sitting on a small table near the door.

> **He sighed. It felt good to have conversations with people who seemed to like talking to him, even if he'd probably never meet them in real life.**

"Time to go to youth group," she said.

Colin tried to tune her out.

She stopped next to his chair. "Colin, let's go."

He couldn't pretend not to hear her anymore. He groaned. "I don't want to."

"Too bad," Mom said back with a chuckle. "You're going."

She was smiling, but he knew she meant what she said. It wouldn't do any good to argue.

Colin slouched into the seat of the car. The church was only a few blocks away. Great for the rest of his family, who were super involved. Not so great for him. If he had a say, he wouldn't be there at all. At least he could avoid talking to anyone by working the sound system—something he'd learned with having a dad and older brother into music. Mom pulled the car around to the back parking lot and let him off outside the door to the youth room. Other kids were arriving and gathering in groups, laughing and talking. Colin felt his whole body stiffen, but he managed to slip by them all. They never looked for him to join them anyway.

Colin stepped behind a black curtain that hid the sound equipment, sat down on a stool, and turned on the system. As the worship band tuned up, he settled into doing what he had to in order to endure the hour. He felt comfortable hidden behind the curtain. He pulled in a breath, his shoulders rising and then falling as he let out a long sigh. His family was involved in everything, it seemed—worship, Bible studies, women's and men's groups, almost every special event. His parents hoped he would get just as involved—and like it.

He didn't.

The worship band finished, and Jake, one of the youth leaders, stepped up to give a message. Colin adjusted the volume for the mic. When he was sure the sound was balanced, he relaxed on his stool.

> **As the worship band tuned up, he settled into doing what he had to in order to endure the hour. He felt comfortable hidden behind the curtain.**

Jake began his lesson for the night. "We see in Jesus' life that relationships matter. They are like these interconnecting chains."

From where he was sitting, Colin couldn't see the youth leader but knew that, as usual, he was holding up something to show the group. Object lessons—Jake's style.

"Each of these represents a different kind of relationship Jesus had with someone else. Or the relationships *we* each have with others."

Colin thought about his relationships. The list wasn't long. His eyes burned with threatening tears. Though it wasn't needed, he reached down and nudged a slider to adjust the sound balance.

The volume went up louder for Jake's next words. "Our family. Friends. Those we know at school or church. Our teachers, our neighbors . . ."

Neighbors. Colin let his youth leader's voice fade into the background of his thoughts. The Jennings family that lived next door to his family—they were more than neighbors to Colin. He had spent so much time with them over the past three years that they were more like family. Lissa was his age, and she had younger brothers. They all hung out, played games indoors and out all year long.

Colin shifted on the stool. *Wish I was there right now.*

Mr. and Mrs. Jennings included him at times when their family went out to eat or even on trips like camping on the beach. He could be himself with them, feel comfortable pretty much no matter what they were doing. But they went to a different church. Colin's shoulders lifted and fell with another sigh.

Jake's voice took on a wrapping-up-the-message tone, and Colin's attention shifted to the sound board again. As the group began a concluding song, he tensed. *How do I get out of here without talking to anyone?*

The next night Colin was online looking up sites on video game trends and strategies. He'd just come from spending several hours at the neighbors' playing Super Smash Bros. His favorite character was Ness, a boy wearing a striped shirt and a baseball cap—a classic character, supposedly well liked by other characters within the game itself and possessing supernatural powers. Colin had battled the afternoon away saving the world from evil.

> ## As the group began a concluding song, he tensed. *How do I get out of here without talking to anyone?*

It was fun, but now he was bored. He wandered into a chat room, signing on with his skater screen name.

sk8n4christ: hey
crashin118: hey what's going on?
sk8n4christ: not much

Colin kept clicking through some sites and then checking the chat.

sk8n4christ: know any good sites for checking out video games?
crashin118: yeah i got one for you.

Comments popped up from others in the chat room while Colin waited. Then an address appeared in the browser dialogue from crashin118.

"great . . . thanks," Colin typed.

He clicked on the URL and started checking out the site's strategies and cheat sheets for different games. He clicked around looking for the one he needed. A pop-up ad opened and

Colin closed it. Just as he found the link for the game strategy he wanted, another pop-up flashed on the screen—a picture of a woman with clickable words blinking, *"Want to get to know me?"* It wasn't the first time he'd seen an invitation, but he'd ignored them before.

Colin paused a moment then shrugged. *Why not?*

> ## *"Want to get to know me?"*
> ## It wasn't the first time he'd seen an invitation, but he'd ignored them before.

He clicked. Pictures popped up showing a barely dressed woman. It looked like her hair was blown back. She was posed in a way that his curiosity was stirred, and he clicked to open another picture . . . then another. *Wow, they're pretty.* Excitement rippled through Colin, then uncertainty over what he was feeling. He found himself swallowing in a nervous sort of way. Colin heard a noise from somewhere else in the house and quickly closed the browser window.

It was just a couple of clicks. Just a few moments.

He stepped away from the computer. He didn't realize what he now dragged with him into the next day and the next—or the toll that the weight of it would begin to take on his thoughts.

> ## Excitement rippled through Colin, then uncertainty over what he was feeling.

> With persuasive words she led him astray;
> she seduced him with her smooth talk.
> All at once he followed her
> like an ox going to the slaughter,
> like a deer stepping into a noose
> till an arrow pierces his liver,
> like a bird darting into a snare,
> little knowing it will cost him his life.
>
> Proverbs 7:21-23

Captured

E-mail. Looking up video game information. Chatting. Mild stuff. But the draw of the Internet was growing strong for Colin. He felt misunderstood, put down, ignored by peers at school and at church—so he figured he didn't need them. Too much thinking about it stirred hurt and longing inside, so online friendships began to work for him. Those he met there responded to him, seemed to be glad to be chatting with him, were interested in what he had to say. They didn't judge him.

Colin quickly found it easy to maneuver around the Internet, and learning anything new became natural. He never would have guessed where any of this would take him, never imagined it could become a problem.

When asked if he had been aware of what it was becoming for him, he said, "I was just captured by being online. What I was doing while I was getting deeper and deeper felt so normal, I thought nothing of it."

Normal for Colin and many like him.

His "deeper and deeper" would grow to involve many aspects of the Internet culture, including hours of gaming, but one trap was far too accessible—pornography. One pop-up. The first click. Pretty accidental, and what he looked at was even mild compared to most. But once drawn in, Colin became trapped. He chose to return to it again and again.

When asked how viewing pornography turned from accidental to eventually becoming a big part of his online obsessions, he said, "More opportunity. More clicks. . . . It got harder to resist."

The first click took him to just a few pictures—he clicked in and then out. Unfortunately, it's nearly impossible for most who look once to stop there. For Colin, the search for pornography quickly became purposeful. Early on, he went to sites where he could find pictures. Then he wanted more and more.

"Later it progressed to sites with videos or stories or games," he said. That eventually included experimentation with cybersex. Looking back, he sees today that at first it wasn't something he wanted to stop *or* that he felt guilty about. He knew his parents wouldn't like it, but he said, "At the time, I thought nothing of it." Guys did this stuff, he thought.

We live in a culture where the lines defining pornography are constantly blurring. Seductively dressed women and men are plastered across billboards or appear in ads that show up nearly anywhere. TV shows in which models walk runways in lingerie are basically public displays of soft porn. Even what we wear on the street, to school, or work can be seductive while also being considered socially acceptable. It's right in front of our eyes almost daily, on the Internet, TV, or in other media. A few clicks looking at something not too different from what you see everywhere else can seem harmless or even "normal."

It isn't harmless. Soft or hard core, pornographic images sink their claws into the mind and cause powerful changes and cravings that become similar to a response to a gateway drug—you gotta go back for more. And it's not just guys—girls can struggle too.

Now, looking back, Colin knows it's huge. "Pornography is the easiest thing for anyone to be lured into. It's common, but no one talks about it. It's such a dark place on the Internet. One pop-up can lead to a click. And one click can mess you up for a long time." Even today, at times, he feels the pull of seduction and fights to master his thoughts.

> With the teens and young adults you know, start a dialogue about how, in any area of our lives, those first choices matter. Talk about what personal situations can make us more vulnerable to poor or dangerous choices. Plan ways to encourage and help each other stay on track.

GETTING IN DEEP

Emotional need. Loneliness. Opportunity.

For Colin, those elements created the perfect storm that sucked him quickly toward compromise. One click, then another, and another.

Nate's loss of a good friend and his strong interest in art gradually led him to porn. Johan and Mike's draw toward pornography began with the print media. The easy access to it online only drew them in further. Ryan and Tyler were like many others: they didn't expect to get pulled in, but the porn was there, easy to find. "We're bombarded with these images online whether we want it or not," Tyler said.

Pornography is seen as one of the heavier online traps, but other seemingly harmless activities, such as gaming and social networking or even researching or other Internet pastimes, can become a trap—our own "first clicks." Before we know it, a large chunk of our time and thoughts have become consumed by these activities. Tyler found himself pulled hard into playing one of the popular MMORPGs (massively multiplayer online role-playing games). "I was playing it all the time—periodically throughout the day and then until four in the morning. It was an idol for me."

Katy enjoys chat rooms and social networking sites. Her clicks pulled her into an online relationship she later regretted. "I found the more time I spent talking to the guy in the chat room, I began to bond myself to him emotionally without really knowing it."

Elize easily lost track of time chatting and Facebooking. But her clicks also gravitated toward spending money. "Shopping and gambling are big problems for me," she said. Now in her twenties, she recognizes her struggle: "I spend way too much money online because I can't feel it physically going out of my hand."

The Internet is huge, the places to go limitless. With a hand on the mouse, we make one choice after another, often with no thought of risk. But the Internet is a strange mix of freedom and danger. As simple and easy as a click of the mouse is, it's just as quick and easy to make split-second decisions that suck us into activities beyond our ability to handle. Sometimes beyond anyone's ability.

We'll never go back to a non-technological time. But we can go forward with a stronger awareness that one click in the present does matter greatly. Each one shapes our perceptions of life and God and our relationships right now and in the future. Each decision, each click *does* matter.

> **Raise the awareness factor in the groups you lead or hang out with. Talk about online use, the impact of our choices, and the responsibility to use the Internet wisely. Do something a little crazy or offbeat like holding a poster contest on Internet responsibility. Use the posters to start a discussion, to get people talking.**

The Choice Is Yours

Johan, one of those mentioned earlier, who struggled with pornography, found his pop-up blocker helped keep his thoughts in check. Still, his eyes could wander toward a strategically placed banner. And yet he says he cannot pass the blame. He knows where he looks is a choice *he* makes. He put it this way: "Internet technicians have not yet found a way of manipulating my neurons and forcing me to click my mouse."

What would it be like if technicians *had* found a way? Or maybe something more sinister—a deliberate plan to deceive you and draw you into a trap.

Imagine this: You sit down at your desk and click on an icon to go online. Not only does your computer connect to the Internet, *you* do. The neurons in your body buzz like the live wires that bring electricity into your home. As you open the browser window, while you are guiding your movements online, other messages from some unknown entity come flowing in, directing what you click on, controlling what you see and what you do. In this scenario, once you connect, decisions are no longer only yours to make.

With one click and then another and another, you go places you never intended. Before you know it, you want more and more—more pictures, more interaction, more games, more adventure, more . . . you fill in the blank. You begin to let go of choice and control.

How very real all this becomes when our online activities take over to that extreme. Obsessions are like that—they control us. And there is no one who would be more happy to have us caught in this trap than the enemy of God, named Satan in the Bible. He is also well known as a deceiver. He began his twisted mission to destroy our relationship with God with the first man and woman—Adam and Eve—and he continues to attempt to do that. He is a master at luring people into traps with attractive or seductive lies. Lowering our guard, thinking we're safe, getting close to that line we think we'd never cross— all provide the perfect opportunity for his work.

So our choices online matter greatly.

True, many of our clicks simply accomplish tasks, but others can impact our souls. What we see and do online enters our minds and can flow right into our hearts. When we step away from the monitor, what we did online is now a part of us.

In the first chapter, we looked at Jesus' words when he said, "Blessed are the poor in spirit." He said those words on a mountaintop in Galilee, giving the greatest sermon ever preached. At that time, he also said, "Blessed are those who hunger and thirst for righteousness, for they will be filled" (Matthew 5:6). At that moment, when Jesus spoke those words, he knew the enticements the people of that day wrestled with, but he also knew, even then, all the offerings that would tug at *your* mind and heart.

Every day, offline and on, work toward longing deeply for what is right and God-honoring—for your own well-being and also for your relationship with God. That's something worth allowing to flow into every part of who you are. The more you find your satisfaction and fullness in him, the choices you make about where to go online will be different.

God, I go online and do my thing, and I walk away—often without realizing how much of what I do there becomes a part of who I am or how I think. I pray for freedom from those clicks that have turned into something that have too strong a hold on my life. Help me to have a passion to know you well. I want to long for a stronger relationship with you rather than longing for what I find online that can never fill my deepest needs. AMEN.

> I will praise the Lord, who counsels me;
> even at night my heart instructs me.
> I have set the Lord always before me.
> Because he is at my right hand,
> I will not be shaken.
>
> PSALM 16:7, 8

GOING DEEPER

■ Think about your own story of Internet use—how you started and what it has become for you today. What would you identify as your "first clicks" into activities that might be starting to control you?

■ Looking at those activities that may be controlling you, what are some specific ways you see that they shape how you spend your day, your perspective on things, or your relationships?

■ It's a huge deal to acknowledge that you're caught up in something that seems like it's starting to control you. Who in your offline world can you honestly talk with about your online choices and what you want to do differently?

DEEPER STILL

Spend some time each day reading the Bible; start a Scripture and prayer journal. Write down verses that stand out to you and show you more about yourself and about God. Then write a prayer to God, asking him to help you understand those verses and apply them in your life. It can be a great habit to review the Scriptures and prayers you've written before you go online.

three

*The Internet was something I felt I could have control over,
no matter how little that control really was in the big scheme of things.*

COLIN STROKED THE LEOPARD'S BACK and thought he sensed tension rippling through its muscles. Or maybe it was his own fear rising up inside. He knew this was a risky move.

The trainer had been walking the leopard through the wild animal park. While he was distracted with visitors asking questions, Colin had approached from behind. The leopard's leash was tight and pulled close to the trainer's side—no guarantee he wouldn't turn on them both. Colin only needed a moment. That was all he had. So far the others in his youth group hadn't noticed he'd stepped away.

Yeah, I'll show them.

He rested his hand lightly on the leopard. *Focus. You can do this.*

> The muscles across his leopard's back danced with grace and power as he paced among the group. No one moved. No one screamed.
>
> http://

He felt the change inside, at first slowly. An electric current seemed to buzz through his hand and spread to his head and legs. Then it happened. In the next instant he had morphed *into* a leopard. The animal he'd been stroking cowered; then the trainer, startled, shielded himself. Colin, now a leopard with tight, rippling muscles, turned and leaped toward where the others from his youth group stood.

"Colin."

The muscles across his leopard's back danced with grace and power as he paced among the group. No one moved. No one screamed. They were too frightened. Now he could beat them at their games.

"Colin."

No no, that wasn't quite the scenario he wanted. Maybe he'd try morphing into something small—a lizard or a bird, like the main character in the book he was reading. *Then I could hide and listen in on conversations without being noticed and—*

"Colin!" A firm, persistent voice broke through his thoughts. Colin rolled over on his bed and saw his mom standing at the door.

"I'm going to the store. Check on Chris while I'm gone."

> Chris couldn't move around quickly or talk like other kids, but Colin usually knew instinctively what he wanted. He understood Chris as much as or maybe better than anyone.

"OK." He slid over to the side of his bed and sat up, still holding the book. He let his fingers slip out of the pages and turned it over to view the cover. It showed a boy about his age, with graduated pictures of the boy morphing into a lizard. He sighed. *Man, it'd be great to be able to do that—to mess with people's minds, to stand up to them.*

Mom poked her head in again, keys in her hand. "OK, I'm leaving. I'll be back in less than an hour. Chris is in his room. Just check on him once in a while.

"Alright." Colin tossed the book onto his bed.

When Mom needed to go somewhere or run errands, he often watched Chris, who needed constant care. Chris couldn't move around quickly or talk like other kids, but Colin usually knew instinctively what he wanted. He understood Chris as much as or maybe better than anyone. And he didn't mind watching him—most of the time.

He got up and walked to Chris's room. His brother was sitting on his bed, playing.

"Hey, Chris, whatcha doing?"

Chris spun the dial on his toy phone. When the eyes on the face moved and it made its ringing sound, Chris looked up at Colin, smiled, and laughed. Chris seemed to love anything that made noise. He looked content for now, so Colin returned to his room.

Rolling back onto his bed, he stretched out on his side and opened his book again. He flipped to the chapter where he'd left off. The main character was approaching a battle and beginning to morph. Colin's mind wandered, and he began thinking about his RuneScape avatar and where he'd last left him in the game.

He drew his thoughts toward the book, and after a few pages they slid back to his game. He'd battled and fought the goblins and thieves but never seemed to gain enough strength to fight the dragon. Strategies began to pulse through his mind. He turned the pages of his book, barely noticed them, hardly read any of the words. His mind was racing: *I need to fight off the evil wizards and get to the top of the tower. Maybe then I'd get what I need to gain more strength.*

He felt edgy. He wanted to play. He got up and went to the kitchen. As he connected to the Internet, in his mind he ran his avatar along the rectangular patterns in the kitchen tile. The computer finally connected, and he opened the game. Once online, he clicked to advance his character through the rooms and levels, at times chatting with other players.

> **Strategies began to pulse through his mind. He turned the pages of his book, barely noticed them, hardly read any of the words. His mind was racing.**

Colin felt a rush. He was fighting his enemies, making progress as he moved up through the tower. He was in charge, taking control.

He sighed. *Control.* It was something he seldom felt he had in real life.

The next night Colin was at youth group—the last place he wanted to be, as usual. The youth leader, Jake, and some of the other kids were arranging chairs into a circle. The room vibrated with the noise of the group—laughing and talking and getting ready for the activity Jake had planned.

"OK, we're going to play Shuffle Your Buns."

Colin drew back while the other kids raced to claim a chair or to sit next to their friends. There were enough seats for everyone—except for the person in the middle of the circle. Colin sat in a chair outside the circle and pulled his cap down toward his eyes.

"Come on, Colin," Jake urged. "You too."

Colin crossed his arms and shook his head no. Some of the kids tried to encourage him. "Come on, man. We're waiting for you." Others groaned and rolled their eyes. "He's not going to. He never does."

Jake walked over and put his hand on his shoulder. "Join us this time, Colin."

> **Tension poured through his throat and landed with a thud in his stomach. He swallowed. If only he could be that leopard now, he'd escape.**

Colin liked his youth leader. He knew what Jake was doing, trying to help, but he didn't want to do this. His stomach tightened. All eyes were on him. He swallowed hard, slid out of his chair, and took the one remaining empty seat in the circle. Tension poured through his throat and landed with a thud in his stomach. He swallowed. If only he could be that leopard now, he'd escape.

"OK, Trevor, you start." Jake stepped away from the circle that was about to explode with activity. Trevor stood in the middle, eyeing the scene around him.

Colin braced himself. In this game you had to keep moving and slide one way or the other onto the next chair in the circle while the person standing in the middle watched for an open chair. He really didn't want to do this.

Trevor was braced, ready for action. He faked them out a couple of times, stepping forward and then drawing back. Then he went for it.

Everyone started shifting around the circle while Trevor darted to find an empty chair. He landed on top of Colin, but before he got off and moved on, his elbow jabbed hard into Colin's chest. It hurt. Colin kept moving with the shuffling group but wished Trevor would hurry up and find an open spot. He wanted the game to end.

Trevor dove into an empty chair. Squeals and laughter pierced the air as everyone shifted to slide onto an available spot. Colin already had his own. As the motion settled, he felt the ache in his chest from Trevor's elbow. Everyone was still laughing. He wasn't. He got up and dropped down onto his chair in the corner of the room again.

> *Yeah this guy has his share of problems, but he can morph anytime he wants to— turn into an osprey and fly away.*

Jake stepped toward the circle. "Let's do it again. Brittany, you're the one falling off the chair. Maria has it. You take the center."

Colin adjusted his cap, crossed his arms, and with his legs scooted his chair back further, closer to the wall. *Wish I could disappear.* Jake looked his way but didn't push for him to stay in the game.

Youth group—one more thing in his life he had little choice about.

Once home he went straight to his room. He wanted to go online—chat, play RuneScape, look up video game codes. He kicked a pile of clothes lying on the floor—they belonged to his oldest brother, who he shared his room with. *Why do Mom and Dad have to limit my time on the computer anyway?* He worked a RuneScape strategy in his mind, but his thoughts slid to the Shuffle Your Buns game at youth group. He felt a sickening feeling return. *Stupid game.*

> **Photo shots and sexual stories of a girl lured him into another world—one where he was accepted. Even more, he was desired.**

He grabbed his book and began to read. *Yeah this guy has his share of problems, but he can morph anytime he wants to—turn into an osprey and fly away.* As he turned page after page, he was pulled into the adventure.

Then Colin noticed the quiet. *Mom and Dad are asleep.* He slid off the bed, checked for sounds down the hall, and snuck toward the kitchen. His heart beat hard. *I don't want to get caught.*

three

He sat down at the computer and connected to the Internet, jumping when the modem screeched and pierced the quiet. *Be cool—they won't hear.* Once he'd assured himself, he let out the breath he held. *Just an hour. That's all I want.* Turning the sound off, he played RuneScape, excitement coursing through him as the strategies he'd worked in his mind played out on the screen. *Yes!*

He stopped and listened for the quietness of the house again.

Just a little bit more.

He closed the game and clicked open a site he'd visited before. Photo shots and sexual stories of a girl lured him into another world—one where he was accepted. Even more, he was desired. She was real—at least for the moment he let his mind go there. He felt his deep loneliness begin to fade. A noise somewhere at the back of the house made him jump. He quickly closed the page and turned off the computer. That was all he could get in for tonight.

He'd take what he could get, but he always hoped for more.

> **Whoever drinks the water I give him will never thirst.**
> **Indeed, the water I give him will become in him a spring**
> **of water welling up to eternal life.**
>
> John 4:14

Colin's online activities seemed to provide an acceptable filler for the thirsty cracks and empty places in his life. What he found on the Internet was accessible, controllable, and interesting. In his real world, relationships, school, and church felt uncomfortable and forced.

Looking back he said, "I couldn't choose whether I went to school—I had to. I couldn't choose not to go to church—parents made me. I had a limited number of friends, and they kinda chose me, not the other way around. And since they were the only people willing to hang out with me, I had no control over that."

The computer he used was still in the kitchen, his use of it still monitored to an extent. But he made his way online anytime he could. "I was going online for longer periods of time, easily hours at a time. A lot of it was done either when my parents were gone or when they thought I was sleeping."

Lonely, hurting, and longing for more than real life seemed to be offering, Colin connected more and more to the Internet while at the same disconnecting from life. When asked what would have made a difference, he said it would have helped to have friends who cared. He added, "I mean, I'm sure my friends were concerned, but they just didn't see what was going on in my life. It's not their fault—who would at eleven or twelve years old? But none of the adults saw it either."

Though his parents and youth workers tried to get him more involved in home and church life, they watched him choose to withdraw. Doug, Colin's dad, pushed hard at first, but in seeing the tension it caused between them, backed off. Terry, his mom, was concerned and at the same time saw a little of herself in Colin. She thought he'd work it through and be OK.

Both of Colin's parents admit they didn't give him a choice about attending church, but from their perspective, they didn't hear a lot of verbal protests from Colin. Terry said that Colin never said much, but she definitely sensed the attitude: *I don't really want to go, but if I have to I will. I'm here because you're making me, not because I want to go.*

His dad, Doug, added, "What's the saying? You can put me in the corner, but you can't beat me down? For us it was the other way around. We were trying to get him to enjoy life, but he wanted to stay in the corner."

Mike, youth pastor at the time, said, "I met with his parents and we talked to Colin. We were never able to isolate why, but he would be emotionally overwhelmed with the whole atmosphere. Seemed like a lot of times that would happen during game time, sometimes during worship—times when you would expect someone would have fun. He would kind of disappear into the back of the room—the corner—and literally just sit in a ball, but couldn't really explain what was up. Those were intense years for him in that regard, and it was tough to know how to help him."

One of the youth leaders often asked Colin how he was doing with his quiet times with God. Colin always gave the same answer: "I don't have one." Colin remembers, "He'd always press me and ask me why until I was very annoyed. I didn't like it, but at the same time I knew it was good that someone was keeping me accountable. Or at least trying."

Thinking more about what might have helped at that time in his life, Colin says, "A better relationship with God—or one at all, for that matter."

> Be assured that someone who is withdrawing has some real needs and, likely, deep hurts. Get to know him. Connect with him as a friend or help him connect with others who are compassionate and patient. Look for some things you can do together that have nothing to do with being online.

REAL NEEDS

Colin wasn't aware the Internet was filling a gap for real needs in his life. It just seemed to him, at first, like something to do, a place to connect and hang out. But for many, like Colin, the Internet becomes a place to go to when lonely, frustrated, or hurting—when their face-to-face relationships and their lives are too painful to deal with. A few dug deeper into the reasons they go online:

Sometimes I use my online buddies as my escape. I just feel empty inside. I need someone who will listen to me.

I get drawn in because talking to friends online is fun. It's a way to get in touch with people who aren't annoying me when other people are.

I could get rid of all my insecurities and be who I wanted to be. I didn't have to worry about messing up or being rejected.

It felt good to be winning at something.

My real heart's cry was for intimacy.

The last one was from Johan, who freely admits to an addiction to porn that began when he was a teen. But while some sites on the Internet claim what they provide is satisfaction for needs that aren't being met, Johan believes these places only feed the isolation. "We need other human beings to keep us grounded and connected and to keep us honest," he said. "People can cause pain, but they offer real perspectives and call our bluff."

Ryan often spent six or seven hours a day online, at times deep into the night. He had painful reasons behind those long hours on the Internet. "I was given up for adoption when I was one and a half. When my adopted parents were able to have a child, they didn't want me anymore." He moved back in with his birth mom, who had remarried, but his stepdad said he didn't want him. He met his birth dad at age fourteen, and Ryan was once again pushed away. "No one really wanted me. I was a burden on everyone's life."

About the Internet, Ryan said, "It's always there when things around you are absent. When there's no real structure and support, you go online looking for your structure and support. It's not going to abandon you. You feel like you can control what happens to you there." But he soon found that the Internet was controlling *him* as he became more and more consumed in networking sites, online war games, and porn.

Kelly said, "It was easier for me to express myself with strangers I couldn't actually see rather than with kids at school who had always made fun of me because I wasn't expressing myself in a way that meshed with what they thought was cool. Plus appearances online didn't matter. When I was younger, I thought I was ... um ... ugly—I don't know how else to say it. I didn't feel like people online were judging me based on how I looked." As she went into high school and continued to struggle with friendships, she began looking more to her online friends for support and companionship.

Katy also turned to the Internet for relationships, especially with guys. She said, "For me it's a security and attention issue. I need to know that my dad loves me. I have a dad in my life, but it's like when I log into the chat room and one or two of my guy buddies start flirting with me, I really like it. They give me the attention I need and the security that I can talk to them and just be myself. I know that I have God and that he is the best Daddy a girl could possibly have, but I just get this nagging feeling that there should be more than this, that my real dad should be more involved with my life."

We long for the connections and closeness of the people in our lives, for their unshakable acceptance of who we are. We want someone to care about what matters to us, to listen and hear us. And with all the crazy stuff that happens in the world, it would be really nice if we could make sense of a few things, maybe have some choice in some of what happens.

When real life seems to be scary, difficult, or lacking, we think, *Why not the Internet?* It seems to be there for us when other people and things aren't. It makes us feel we can choose, we can escape, we can fight, and sometimes we can even win.

But are we winning? And if it seems that we are, at what cost?

Navigating real-world relationships and pressures while trying to grow comfortable with who you are can be tough. Dialogue about those challenges and how they influence online choices and identities.

WHO YOU ARE

You've seen them. For many chats, message boards, online communities, and role-playing games, you can choose a graphic image to represent yourself in the online world—the avatar or the gravatar. And you decide how close to your actual self you want the online image to be.

Graphics can never be more than a symbolic image. No matter how much technology or science advances, no one—especially ourselves—can create an exact representation of who we are.

But in a really amazing way, God did that with himself. He was fully represented as God-in-the-flesh in Jesus. Hebrews 1:3 says: "The Son is the radiance of God's glory and the exact representation of his being, sustaining all things by his powerful word." Jesus is an *exact* representation. A perfect expression. Truly and fully God. And he stepped into our world to live life among his created people—so we could know him.

He loves us that much. He cares about every insult, rejection, hurt, or abandonment we've experienced. He knows, on the deepest level, what sends us running, hiding, or escaping when the real world has left us feeling we can't handle it anymore. He knows about the deterioration of the soul that spins a person toward abandoning his or her relationship with him and instead settling for substitutes to satisfy distorted passions.

He knows. And he weeps.

So he stepped into our world—God as man—to battle for souls. He battled for yours and for mine, and he gave his life.

And about images and representations—did you know that next to Jesus, of all creation, we are the closest to being made in God's image? God said it himself. Genesis 1:26: "God spoke: 'Let us make human beings in our image, make them reflecting our nature'" (*The Message*).

When Jesus looks at you, that is what he sees—you stamped with the image of God. You matter to him. All your insecurities, longings, struggles, darkest secrets, and hidden pain . . . matter.

See yourself in that loved image, your identity wonderfully real. That's who you can be as you connect with him.

God, being online is a part of life, but there are ways I turn to it to fill the empty gaps in my life. When I am hurt and lonely or even bored, give me the strength to turn away from seeking fulfillment in empty online substitutes. Show me all of who you are and what that means for who I am as someone created in your image. Let the reality of that identity sink deep into my days and impact my confidence and my choices on every level. AMEN.

> You're blessed when you're content with just who you are—
> no more, no less. That's the moment you find yourselves
> proud owners of everything that can't be bought.
>
> MATTHEW 5:5 (*THE MESSAGE*)

GOING DEEPER

- It's possible that the deep hurts and questions you have when facing the real world offline are a part of what sends you to your online activities or escapes. What is going on in your life that has been difficult, confusing, or hurtful?

- We might be aware that our online choices are based in interests or passions that we've taken in directions we know don't honor God or who he made us to be. Do you see that happening? Write some about that here, or discuss it with a friend.

■ How can you begin to see yourself as loved and made in God's image? List a few ways right now.

DEEPER STILL

Meet with your pastor, youth pastor, or a community ministry leader and talk about ways you can use your talents and gifts to help them and serve others. Ask them for their assistance in developing a project that you can do over the next month or so, or even over the next semester. Use your computer skills in supportive ways to help bring it about.

four

I spent most of my time either on a computer or thinking about being on one. I couldn't get enough.

"Wow, that's cool, Colin. How'd you do that?"

"What'd he do? Let me see."

Colin dropped his hand away from the computer and leaned back as his junior high classmates gathered around his computer station to look at the screen. He'd added a few more touch-ups to the site he was working on, and it was now looping a song clip he'd found online. The class was learning HTML and designing websites. Most of the students had only figured out how to get a few basic lines of information up on their sites.

"Yeah, how'd you do that?"

Colin grinned. More students crowded in to see.

"Where'd you find the music clip?"

"What's the code for getting it to loop like that?"

Colin hadn't planned to stir up interest in his site. The guy who sat next to him started it. He'd been looking at the site the school used for uploading student work. When he opened Colin's page, the song began to play, and he wanted to know how to do it.

"OK, everyone, return to your seats, and we'll cover some netiquette." Mr. Berry, in his out-of-style brown cords and plaid flannel shirt, moved to the front of the computer stations. Some of the students groaned as they headed back to their seats.

Colin closed his page and the song stopped. The clip was from a video game song that in the game meant you'd received invincibility status. Colin blew out a sigh. *If only I had that invincibleness.*

He felt a tap on his shoulder. It was a guy who, as far as he could remember, had never spoken to him before. "Hey, could I get the code from you for that later?" The guy gave him a big grin.

"Sure."

"Cool."

> **The clip was from a video game song that in the game meant you'd received invincibility status. Colin blew out a sigh.**
> *If only I had that invincibleness.*

"Alright, everyone to your seats *now*." Mr. Berry turned toward the whiteboard, picked up an erasable marker, and wrote "SHOUTING" in all caps. "When you're e-mailing or posting to groups, writing in all capital letters is like shouting." He raised the volume of his voice a notch.

"And we don't want to shout," someone whispered behind Colin in a mocking tone. Others laughed in low tones, trying to keep it to themselves. A lot of the students made fun of Mr. Berry. Colin liked him, but sometimes his lectures got boring. Like now. Colin's thoughts wandered.

He was doing well in the class. This one and band class seemed to be the only ones he could nail. The others would probably be OK if he tried harder and finished the homework. But he didn't care *that* much. Computer stuff came easy.

His thoughts shifted. He thought about how he almost didn't take the class. He'd had a girlfriend—his first. She was taking the class, so he signed up too. Then she dropped it . . . and him.

Dumped by e-mail. Couldn't she have just told me to my face? On second thought, better that she didn't. Would have been worse in person.

He'd been bummed ever since—really bummed. But he'd stayed in the class. Every day he was learning new things and devouring them. He could pour his focus into this.

Colin dropped his backpack on his bed and sat down in front of the computer. *His* computer. No more sharing the kitchen computer. No more dial-up. Now they had high-speed—an immediate connection whenever he wanted. He smiled and brought his fist down through the air. "Yes."

> *Dumped by e-mail. Couldn't she have just told me to my face? On second thought, better that she didn't.*

He got online and joined a chat where he always seemed to find the girl who constantly talked about Justin Timberlake or the guy who tried to pick up on girls, asking their age, sex, and location with the question "asl?" Colin read their comments, rolled his eyes, then checked his e-mail. He continued to add his

four

own comments to the chat while he looked for ways to change up his site design.

As he inserted new code, he thought about the day, how his classmates were now asking *him* how to create effects on their sites. *Yeah, guess it was an OK day for a change—good as they get anyway.* He was way ahead of everyone in computer class, and he didn't mind helping. He felt needed and that felt good.

Mostly.

In the wait between comments in a chat, he thought about the guys in his class who only talked to him when they wanted something. Outside of class was worse; they would just ignore him. He shook away the growing ache he felt inside and turned his attention back to the screen.

In the wait between comments in a chat, he thought about the guys in his class who only talked to him when they wanted something.

He switched to playing a real-time-strategy war game, where he could chat and strategize while he played. Fifteen minutes turned into two hours. As he pushed away from the computer to grab something to eat, his mind stayed in game track. In his head, he worked out his next moves for the game. As he walked down the hall, his thoughts jumped to what he wanted to try on his site and the code that would make it work. He entered the kitchen and clicked into thinking of what he'd look up next.

Mom came in through the sliding door and asked if he'd help with Chris.

"Just watch him in the back yard for a few minutes while I finish making his meal shake."

He didn't mind. He stepped outside. Picking up a ball, he rolled it to Chris. His brother laughed, grabbed the ball, and tried to roll it back. Colin knew his brother loved him, and he loved Chris more than just about anyone.

"Yeah, Chris, if it weren't for you I may not have all that much patience with others." He heaved out a sigh and thought of his classmates. *If only they appreciated me as much as you do.* He felt tension building up in his chest, sadness twisting his stomach. He felt himself spinning toward a despair he knew too well. Fear chased after him. *I don't want to go there. I don't know how to get out. Gotta shake this off.*

Colin rolled the ball again, then stood and paced. His thoughts edged back to what he'd been doing online. He looked toward the door and saw that Mom had Chris's meal ready.

As soon as he returned to his room, he slid right into his game as if he'd never left. Didn't notice he'd skipped his dinner. Drawn in, he became one with the avatar he controlled, running the fields, fighting the enemy, feeling the exhilaration of the victories, the disappointment of the defeats. He was unaware of his heart beating faster, adrenalin pushing him to fight harder. He was once again immersed, pulled in and leaving the real world far behind.

> I don't want you ending up in blind alleys,
> or wasting time making wrong turns.
> Hold tight to good advice; don't relax your grip.
> Guard it well—your life is at stake!
>
> PROVERBS 4:12, 13 (*THE MESSAGE*)

IMMERSED

It all started out so naturally—a teen going online. Except now Colin was fighting two monsters, each feeding on and complicating the other. One was his obsession with computers and the Internet; the other was a growing and gnawing depression.

The adults in his life recognized his struggle with fitting in, saw the sadness. He'd grow out of it, wouldn't he? And his computer interests and spending a lot of time online—that was common enough with teens. Besides, it seemed to be one thing Colin enjoyed, even felt good about.

Now at age twenty-one, Colin looks back and readily admits that by junior high, even before he had a computer in his room, he was addicted to the Internet. He doesn't use that word—addicted—lightly, doesn't laugh about it.

Getting online, gaming, chatting, and checking out sites was constantly on his mind. He said, "I'd think about what I'd do with it when I got home from school—where I'd go next, who I'd fight." And he added, "I was addicted to the Internet before I was addicted to porn. I really realized it was an addiction when it started taking over my thought life." He remembers the progression: "First it was just the Internet, then flashes from porn images came that I couldn't control, and it was distracting me at school, at home, at church, when I was with my friends . . . everywhere."

Colin had stumbled into a large new world that he liked, and he wanted to stay there. "Never through the course of my Internet addiction did I picture it as a bad thing," he said.

Seeing how consuming it became for him, he now says, "You can look like you're functioning, but if it's all you do, it's just another way to step away from life."

> Depression may be a part of why someone turns to the Internet. Know the signs. They include irritability, loneliness, lack of energy, a chronic sense of sadness, or withdrawing. Medical or counseling intervention may be the crucial next step.

AN OVERPOWERING LURE

Colin isn't the only one whose normal online activity turned into an online trap. Tyler said he became addicted to MySpace, WoW, and pornography. "It would feel like I *need* to check my MySpace, or I *need* to play WoW, or I *need* to see who's online. I couldn't go a day without checking my MySpace. I'd wake up and check it, and then check it eight times a day."

Tyler admits he had other online obsessions too. "Pornography was a big part of my addiction. Now I know if I'm even starting to think that I want to look up a pornographic site, I've already crossed the line of spending too much time online. I'm too comfortable."

About World of Warcraft, he says, "There were times when I was almost physically dependent on WoW. It was time-consuming for me, to the point I'd wake up in the middle of the night and play. It became a big part of my life. I'd definitely call it an addiction. WoW—it's so real is the thing. It's almost like it's a second life. I'm thinking about it right now. It's like something is going off in my brain right now, and I want to play because I'm thinking about it."

And yet, Tyler admits, there is an irony: Though he enjoyed the game while playing, it often left him feeling empty. "There were times when I played all day, into the evening, and I'd be lonely at the end of the day. I'd be depressed. But there were also other times when I didn't play, and I'd be depressed because I didn't. Just a vicious cycle."

Tyler was a social guy, so it wasn't that he withdrew from friends like others might. He used a social networking site to check on parties and find drugs. He said, "Addiction to the Internet has been a huge part of my life, but I see how destructive it can be. Not only was I addicted to the Internet, I was supporting other addictions through it."

Others shared their experiences:

Kelly: I lost track of what I was doing. Mostly, it was when I was having a good time or when I was getting into some kind of emotional conversation—whether it was an argument or something else.

Nate: Sometimes I stayed on all night long MySpacing, messaging, with some porn thrown in. I got drained, tired.

Katy: I get done with the computer, I feel drained and lazy like I just don't want to do anything the rest of the day. I think that must mean I'm spending way too much time on nonproductive things.

Ryan: Gaming and MySpace weren't things I thought about only when the computer was in front of me. I thought about them while I was doing other tasks. No trigger around me. Just something that was constantly going through my head. The need for it. And it wasn't just me, but my friends too.

Some of these identified their use as an addiction. They were repeatedly, often increasingly, hooked on some aspect of it. Others, while they wouldn't call their use an addiction, knew they were at least leaning toward overuse or abuse—either in the amount of time spent, how much they thought about it, or what they chose to do there.

Chronic and *compulsive* are two common characteristics of any addiction. It can be a psychological or physiological dependency and can be driven by a need to rev up excitement or reduce tension. And the cycle of trigger, need, and fulfillment just keeps the addiction going until there's intervention.

But the word *addiction* is thrown around a lot, even used jokingly about things we really like. So how do we begin to take our Internet use and choices seriously, with an openness that what we're doing *could* be a problem?

Here's a list of statements compiled from research and interviews with several authors, experts, and youth culture specialists. As you read through these, and in light of the stories above, consider your own use. Keep in mind, even a few of these in your life could be pointing to a situation worth taking a much closer look at.

I think about it or read about it often when not online and anticipate the next online session.

I'm losing interest in other activities I used to do and enjoy.

I choose it more often than other social activities and being with significant people in my life.

I'm online for long periods of time by myself.

I turn to it when I'm hurt, anxious, hopeless, or depressed, more often than to other ways to cope.

I can't think of anything else to do instead.

I feel I *need* it—for excitement, to give me a lift, or for social interactions.

I have a strong defensiveness about my online activities.

I'm willing to lie about the amount of time I spend or what I do online.

I'm irritable when interrupted by real-life relationships and responsibilities.

I consistently choose it over responsibilities like homework or doing chores.

I'm neglecting family and friends more and more.

My use and thoughts about it are affecting my performance in school or on my job.

I get moody, restless, depressed, or frustrated when I can't get online when I want to.

I look forward to being online but become depressed or just feel sluggish afterwards.

I can't get off the computer when I say I'm going to.

I've said I'm going to cut down, but I don't.

I'm beginning to neglect some things—like taking showers or just keeping myself clean.

I'm experiencing changes physically, including in my eating or sleep patterns.[1]

Most experts agree that some individuals are more likely to struggle with Internet addiction. Tom Neven of Focus on the Family, who has studied online use among teens and young adults, said, "There seems to be evidence to support what's called an addictive personality—a personality type that is prone to addictions of many kinds, be they chemical or electronic."

But for any of us, he adds this advice: "Don't be fooled by thinking you're playing only 'safe' games or visiting 'safe' sites. While discerning content is important, it's the *process* of interacting with electronic media that becomes addictive."

Margaret Meeker, physician and author, suggests a scale to identify where you are in your Internet use. At zero you never think about it. A five might be that you think about it . . . and you don't know how or when it's going to happen, but you know you'll end up online soon, or at least try to get online. At ten you can't stop thinking about the next time you'll be on. Meeker said, "It's not about the difference between a seven or an eight, but which end of the scale."

Olivia Bruner, co-author of the book *PlayStation Nation*, said, "If you're saying, 'I've got to have it, and I've got to have

---

1   Contributing experts: Olivia Bruner, co-author with husband Kurt, of *PlayStation Nation*; Dr. Kimberly Young, author of *Caught in the Net* and *Tangled in the Web*; youth culture experts, Walt Mueller of the Center for Parent/Youth Understanding, and Tom Neven of Focus on the Family; Dr. Margaret Meeker, physician and author of *Restoring the Teenage Soul*.

four

it now or today,' you're crossing the line and you're going into addiction. You're not in control anymore. It's in control of you."

It takes courage to take an honest look at your choices and activities—to consider not only what sends you to the Internet but also what now holds you there.

Here's a question to ask yourself or to talk over with someone you know will be honest with you: Is this activity adding value or benefit to my life? Healthy passions and interests add value; addictions or obsessions take away—they rob and drain.

In that sense, they're hurting everyone around you, but especially one person—you.

> One red flag to watch for is changes in personality. For instance, maybe your friend used to be active and loving, but now she's withdrawn and angry or depressed. Don't ignore it, but at the same time, don't assume it's *only* her Internet use. Other issues may be going on too.

SEEING INSIDE

In the middle of an immense lake, the man in the boat fell to his knees in front of another man. The kneeling man had known he was in the presence of someone special—he had called him master—but *holy?* That he hadn't seen before—at least not as he now felt it, deep in his bones. His own naked, depraved soul was exposed. He wanted to run, but he had no place to go.

This is a true story, about a man named Peter, just before he became one of Jesus' disciples. After an exhausting and unsuccessful night of fishing, he and his buddies were on the shores cleaning their nets. And Jesus showed up and told them to take the boats out and let down their nets. Though skeptical, Peter obeyed what Jesus said. When they caught so many fish that the nets began to break and the two boats started to sink, Peter was struck with awe. Here's what the Bible says about his reaction:

"When Simon Peter realized what had happened, he fell to his knees before Jesus and said, 'Oh, Lord, please leave me—I'm too much of a sinner to be around you.' For he was awestruck by the number of fish they had caught, as were the others with him" (Luke 5:8, 9, *NLT*).

To Peter, there was more to his amazement than the great catch. At that instant, Peter caught a revealing glimpse of who Jesus was, and he felt the reality of the stark contrast between himself and God. It brought him to his knees.

Jesus told Peter and the others not to be afraid. He had great things for them to do. They didn't take long to respond. "As soon as they landed, they left everything and followed Jesus" (Luke 5:11, *NLT*).

How might we live differently if we experienced an extraordinary moment of truth where we see our lives held up in contrast to the holiness of God? That's an honesty few are willing to invite. But God longs for us to go before him with our souls naked and open to seeing all that we've become trapped in—not so we will be so struck down we can't get up and live, but with the goal that we can now go forward living more fully and passionately, immersed in the things that count.

Ask God for that honest glimpse.

four

God, it's not easy to be honest with myself or with you or others in my life—especially when I've been pulled into online activities that seem to have me captured in ways I'm reluctant to change. But I'm asking—help me see you not only the way I should but also to see myself the way I should. Give me not only an honest reflection of who I am and what I need but also the courage, strength, and hope to move forward into all you have for me. AMEN.

His mercy flows in wave after wave on those who are in awe before him.

LUKE 1:50 (*THE MESSAGE*)

GOING DEEPER

■ Take time to go through the list in this chapter and consider how you're doing with your Internet use. Consider any ways your activities may be sliding into the excessive zone.

■ Evaluate your openness to take steps to balance your time or face the facts about your activities. Where do you land on the willingness scale? What can you do to bump that up a couple of notches?

■ One way to catch an honest glimpse of where we are is to spend more time with God. Write down a few ways you will commit to daily time with him.

DEEPER STILL

Get with a mentor or good friend who spends regular, deep time with God. Together, using the lists and questions in this chapter, evaluate your online activities and come up with some steps to begin to make changes. Include meeting weekly with your friend for times of prayer and Bible study.

five

I wasn't monitoring my time.
I wasn't making an attempt to be in the real world.
I was pretty shut off and, as a result of that, pretty depressed.

I CAN BEAT THE DRAGON. *I've just gotta gain more experience to level up.*

In his mind, Colin ran his avatar through the battles of RuneScape, still trying to figure out how to master one part of the game that had been difficult for him. He'd played it for six hours the night before and had come so close.

His thoughts jumped to the new message board he'd created. He wanted to tweak the look some more and fix how the messages posted. *Shouldn't be a problem. I just need to . . .* Another thought crashed into his mind. He remembered how he had been browsing a site he had to shut down when his mom came into the room. Thankfully, she always knocked first.

"She's just messing with you."

"What?" Colin jumped. He'd forgotten that he'd been having a conversation with his friend Kevin before his mind wandered toward what was so often on his mind lately. He tugged his attention back toward his friend. "What did you say?"

"I said Lisa is just messing with you. Don't fall for it."

Colin picked up his music sheets and event schedule the high school band teacher had given them and shoved them into his backpack. He didn't answer out loud. *You don't know what you're talking about. Lisa does like me—I can tell.* He thought about the week before when the three of them were hanging out, walking around during lunch period across the back of the school baseball field. Lisa had held his hand and cuddled into him. They were laughing and having a good time. *She even hugged me. You were there, Kevin. You saw it.*

> **Colin jumped. He'd forgotten that he'd been having a conversation with his friend Kevin before his mind wandered toward what was so often on his mind lately.**
>
> http://

His friend pulled his clarinet apart and began laying the sections into his case. "Hey man, I just wanted to give you a heads-up. I've seen her hanging out with some jock, and I'm pretty sure he's her boyfriend."

"Alright, thanks for telling me." Colin didn't want to hear any more. He still didn't believe it. Under his breath he swore, but caught himself before Kevin heard. He pulled his backpack up over his shoulder. "I'll see you later."

He stepped outside and down the cement staircase leading out of the music building. Angling left, he headed across the high school campus toward where he often hung out at lunch—in a small, sheltered patio outside the computer lab.

It was windy and starting to rain. Colin pulled his hood over his head and sped up the pace. A familiar laugh nearby caught his attention, and he looked up just in time to see Lisa passing, her arm hooked in some guy's arm. *Great.* Colin's stomach twisted inside with disappointment. She had made him feel special. How had he fallen for it? *Kevin's right—just playing with me. Should have seen it coming.* Out loud he muttered a few choice swear words and then he shook his head. *But I'm not going to let it get to me.*

He ran under the overhang where the others he knew were already crowded in and sitting on a step or on the cement patio. Swinging his backpack down, he dropped to sit and crossed his long legs in front of him. Already a wide stream of shallow water was forming and flowing from the fields at the back of the school toward a nearby drain. The group huddling out of the rain affectionately called it The River. At times they jokingly referred to it as a holy river that was desecrated when anyone stepped through it.

> *Great.* Colin's stomach twisted inside
> with disappointment.
> She had made him feel special.

"Ah, he's arrived—the unassuming young lad with an uncanny knack for attracting lovely young ladies." Mark was partially quoting from the fantasy novel series by Piers Anthony. He and Colin often stepped into role-playing their own created fantasy characters, either driving their friends to hysterics or driving them crazy.

"Not funny," Colin said, and then remembered Mark had no clue what had just happened with Lisa.

"What's this? Have you lost your abilities? Or are you merely using your preferred power to confuse?"

five

Colin was silent.

"Ohhh-kay. Never mind." Mark left Colin alone and turned his attention to the others, who seemed to be ignoring the two of them anyway. They were discussing their latest ventures in WoW and RuneScape. Some were arranging a time when they could get on the lab computers and play Warcraft in teams.

Colin tuned them out. He didn't feel that close to most of them anyway. It was just a place to hang out, but he did like the shared interest in online games and reading fantasy. He liked anything fantasy. Real life wasn't so great. Escaping to made-up worlds—so much better. There he had abilities he didn't have anywhere else. He could go on adventures.

Adventures.

> **He liked anything fantasy. Real life wasn't so great. Escaping to made-up worlds— so much better. There he had abilities he didn't have anywhere else.**

Plenty of that going on in his family. Except for his brother Chris, who had been really sick and not eating, everyone else seemed to be all wrapped up in something exciting. Dad was studying for a test to try for a new job, and with recent terrorist events, he had new material to get down. Mom had returned to school to study bookkeeping. His oldest brother was off on a mission trip in Africa.

And look at my miserable, boring life. Nothing's happening. The only good thing I have going now is a bedroom to myself where I can really be alone. Works for me. Easy to disappear. No one seems to notice anyway.

One leg was falling asleep, and Colin stretched it out to get the blood flowing again. The conversation continued without him. They seemed to ignore him and only noticed when he didn't laugh as usual at one of their crude jokes.

Mark slugged Colin's arm. "Hey, what's wrong with you?"

"Nothing."

Mark shrugged. "Yeah, right—whatever."

Colin's thoughts slid back to home. With everyone into their own adventures, he felt left out—in the way. It was just as well—he could fade into the background and into his room. At least sometimes, when he felt like it, he could hang out at the Jennings'.

Everyone started moving around, grabbing their stuff, throwing their lunch trash away.

"What's going on?" Mark asked him as they headed out into the stormy weather to get to the next class.

"Life stinks." He was tempted to add a few other choice words.

"Well, yeah, but what's new?" Mark was trying to lighten his mood.

Colin rolled his eyes. "Yeah, really—what *is* new?"

Was it worth going through life like this just to get through it? He wasn't so sure.

At home, Colin sat on the edge of his bed. He could hear his parents talking over what to do next with Chris. They were worried. He wasn't eating and seemed to be shutting down. Since he couldn't communicate, they didn't know what to do.

five

Colin was worried too. He loved Chris and didn't want to lose him. He always protected him from people who teased him, but he couldn't protect him from getting so sick he could die. He pushed off the bed and sat at his desk. He checked his e-mail. He had a few in his inbox, but he felt so tired—so down and alone—he was in no hurry to respond to a few new messages. He listened to the conversation outside his room that traveled down the hall and toward the kitchen. *Does anyone even remember I'm here? Doubt it. I'll just stay in here and be one less thing for them to think about.*

He chatted on AIM and ate up some time doing that. He switched to RuneScape. It took a while to get into it this time. The house grew quiet. The day gave way to night and brought darkness, and the darkness seemed to crowd into his mind.

Life—I'm just going through the motions. Don't want to be here. Want to run . . . escape.

He leaned forward and clicked open a new browser window. He knew where he wanted to go. No one was there to stop him.

http://

Before he could be swallowed up in the sadness, he lost himself deeper into his game. Running his avatar along passageways and conquering levels, he searched for his adventure, groped for purpose. After several more hours he had fought wizards and defeated some, fought dragons and lost to them. But he'd increased his character's power and gained a couple of levels. At least that was something.

He dropped back in his chair. The satisfaction felt flat. His own life was still so lacking in any real adventure, so empty.

Stupid life.

Despair began to wrap its fingers around his mind, drawing him to a dark, lonely place. He panicked.

Don't go there. Stop thinking.

He leaned forward and clicked open a new browser window. He knew where he wanted to go. His brother was far away on a mission trip. No one was there to stop him. *This* was available—right there, offering its own kind of passion and adventure, drawing him away to another place.

Reflected pictures of women flashed in his glasses, their smiles and seduction twisting images into his mind—the porn's deception promising to draw him into soft, welcoming arms, offering satisfaction.

He found himself smiling. *Yeah, I like this.*

Like a street drug, it clamped him into its lustful grasp. It whispered, *"Come on, you can have more and more and more . . ."*

So he went . . . seeking its comfort, its escape. But he knew deep down that it was only sucking more and more life out of him.

My purpose in writing is simply this: that you who believe in God's Son will know beyond the shadow of a doubt that you have eternal life, the reality and not the illusion. And how bold and free we then become in his presence, freely asking according to his will, sure that he's listening.

1 JOHN 5:13, 14 (*THE MESSAGE*)

Emptiness silently consumes. For Colin, it was slowing chewing away at his soul.

By the time he was a freshman entering high school, Colin was just going through the motions, being where he felt others expected him to be. If he could choose, he'd be anywhere else. And so, drawn to fantasy, he continued further into that world. Deeper escape and more adventure became his primary goals.

He'd lose himself in Piers Anthony's world of Xanth and in role-playing conversations with his friend Mark. He didn't view those things as bad activities. He said, "It wasn't destructive. Just part of who I was, escaping from real life." He felt he could stimulate his imagination by reading fantasy and playing the games. "I've always been drawn to that—to think about things that couldn't be."

How easily the innocence and strength of imagination can be turned toward compromise and destructive online fantasy. Porn, endless hours of gaming, multiple virtual relationships—each, in its own way, twists the imagination and ends up tainting the wonder of reality, whether it's fullness of life, depth of relationship, or sex as God intended it.

Colin's online activities were dragging him further and further into the empty black hole of escape. His gaming alone would consume up to six hours a day. And both gaming and pornography now more often took over his thoughts while he lived in the real world.

But the real world was taking a toll on him emotionally. Life wasn't feeling all that fun for Colin, and now he watched his family grow busy pursuing and enjoying new activities. "My depression at that time was caused by a bunch of change happening at once. I felt left out because I wasn't going through an adventure. . . . I was just going to high school." And especially given his aversion to the school atmosphere, that wasn't enough.

Can't have an adventure? Escape to your own, Colin thought. And as long you look busy and seem productive, no one will know how much you're just barely hanging on. Colin said, "In my mind, the Internet was an ideal escape. I could look like I was functioning without anyone questioning it."

No one did. With all that was happening in the family that year, coupled with his quietness, Colin's depression and escape were easy for the family to overlook.

Terrorist threats and other security scares created extra pressures for Colin's dad, who was studying to work with the local police department's emergency system. After the 9/11 terrorist attacks, everyone was scrambling to know how to handle the potential dangers. Doug, Colin's dad, said, "I had all that going on with me, so I was paying like zero attention at home. I was trying to, but I was gone twelve, thirteen hours a day, four days a week. So was I able to focus on Colin at that time? No. I was not even close to doing that."

And for a son who often kept to himself, it was an easy assumption for his dad to make: "Everything's fine."

Chris's mental and health issues also had a bearing. Colin's mom, Terry, realized her needed focus on Chris was a challenge for both of her other sons: "They've had to deal with the fact that Christopher was always a presence, and his problems often loomed more important than theirs."

five

So in the middle of that backdrop, Colin was left to find anything that could bring some excitement into what otherwise seemed a dreary existence. He said, "I never thought of physically escaping my life. It was easier to just log on to the Internet." So he did. Sad and lonely, craving adventure, interaction, and pleasure, he turned even more to the world he'd already found so accommodating.

He had yet to discover that there are far more and better options in life available, adventures that would feed his thirsty soul instead of eating it away.

> **Boredom, insecurities, and difficult family or friendship situations are just some of the things that send teens and young adults deep into an online escape. Watch for ways you can encourage creativity and the development of interests. Provide opportunities to talk through difficulties and engage in solutions.**

ESCAPE

When the deepest part of us is thirsty, empty, the gnawing need inside doesn't let go. We may be willing to accept whatever will quench the longing, even if it means settling for a tainted substitute instead of what would really satisfy and nourish. We go online to escape, to fill a need, to look for excitement. It satisfies only as long as we are there. We stay longer. We go back more.

Tyler said, "I escaped from my family a lot. I'd close the door and lock it so I wouldn't be bothered. I didn't want to deal with things, didn't want to be told to do anything. And there were anger issues going on with my family. If I got in trouble with my mom or dad or my sister, there was my escape—I'd go play WoW." But it never stopped with just a few sessions. "I'd dream about it, play seven hours a day, sometimes through the night."

Ryan, who faced continual rejection from family, turned to the Internet. "It was easy to get away from my problems and not think about what was going on. I could zone out and not worry." He played games, chatted, constantly checked his online profile, and viewed porn. "I'd lose track of time. Next thing I knew, it's 3 AM and I hadn't done anything or had a meaningful conversation. I'd done whatever just to keep myself occupied and stay on the computer."

Pornography became Johan's escape. Looking back, he said, "Porn circumvents the necessity for me to become a student of true love. Porn gives me the 'prize' of pleasure and orgasm without the investment of time, intimacy, and vulnerability. Porn lets me have all the fun without demanding that I grow up."

Growing up is often not an easy road. Sometimes we long for something less complicated or painful than what real life has thrown our way.

Nate said, "I would get away from arguments and discussions with my parents and would escape into looking up art." Then his girlfriend died in a car accident. He said, "I was so lonely, I got into pornography and bad relationships. Loneliness led me into really depressing stuff online."

Friendships were hurtful and complex for Katy, so she began to prefer online friends through chat and social networking sites. "There's no drama. So sometimes I use my online buddies as my escape." But while going online seemed to help her avoid offline drama, Katy found herself emotionally pulled into an online relationship. She got hurt.

Somehow our needs, pain, questions, or desires talk us into believing that escape may be better than reality. That finding relief or satisfaction of our immediate or deepest needs can be as simple as a few clicks. What starts out as a fun pastime or an OK way to cope with a few of life's pressures pulls us in until we are no longer aware or care that our escape has become much more to us. We can't do without it.

But there *is* something more, something far better than we can imagine.

> In groups and one-on-one conversations with others, talk about the beauty of God's creation, his design in creating us, his miracles, and the amazing ways he works. He outmatches anything we can find on the Internet. Create a thirst for him.

SOMETHING TO RUN TOWARD

Online we are amazed by colorful worlds with graphics that not only mimic the real world but seem to outmatch it in creating an experience of impossibilities. We seemingly have no limits to the connections we can make around the world as we chat simultaneously with someone next door, someone in South

Africa, someone in Japan. Each time we go online we see the opportunities and offers: our desires can be satisfied instantly, or at least as quickly as our expertise or Internet connection will allow.

But with all its creativity to awe us, even with its constant stream of innovations and boundless access, it *is* limited. Very limited. Especially in its ability to meet our deepest longings. For those, it can't be more than a substitute—*ever*. God created us with amazing, unmatched intricacy—physically, emotionally, and spiritually. He created *you*. What nourishes your thirsty soul can only come from him.

A writer of one of the psalms spoke of God meeting our inner longings: "You have made known to me the path of life; you will fill me with joy in your presence, with eternal pleasures at your right hand" (Psalm 16:11). Paul, the writer of a letter to the followers of Christ in the city of Ephesus, taught about God's ability to fill our lives: "God can do anything, you know— far more than you could ever imagine or guess or request in your wildest dreams! He does it not by pushing us around but by working within us, his Spirit deeply and gently within us" (Ephesians 3:20, *The Message*).

When you want to run and escape, run to him. With him, you'll experience things that seem like impossibilities made possible. You'll get to know a God who loves you and comes alongside you in your difficult realities. You'll find a lasting satisfaction that is deeper, fuller, and better than anything you've known before, anything you can ever imagine. Don't settle for less.

God, I run to you with all my needs and desires, for only you can satisfy those. When I am lonely or sad, when life is too much, remind me that I can find fulfillment and answers in you and in your Word. You walk alongside me, so I don't need to run away and hide or escape online. Show me when I'm using my online time that way, when I'm not trusting you as I should with my questions and hurts. Help me grow in my confidence that you know and understand and can fill my life up beyond my wildest dreams. AMEN.

**I said to the Lord,
"You are my Lord; apart from you I have no good thing."**
PSALM 16:2

GOING DEEPER

■ Being connected online, by itself, is not a bad thing. But consider a time when you went online desperate for an escape. What happened in your day that made things hard for you and made you feel like you wanted to get away from it all?

■ What are some healthy ways you can respond to what happens in your day or ways you can respond to a desire or need? How can you involve God?

■ Think about the worries and concerns that weigh you down and that could potentially become reasons to escape. Who can you ask to come alongside you, to pray with you, and help you make a plan to handle those?

five

DEEPER STILL

On a large card or half sheet of paper, write these three things:

- something you struggle with that makes you want to escape to an online activity;

- different offline options you can do to help you get through that time or even to resolve it;

- and then—but in bold or large letters—the Scripture, "I can do everything through Christ, who gives me strength" (Philippians 4:13, *NLT*).

Be as creative as you can.

Place the card or half sheet near your computer to remind you what you'll do next time you're tempted to escape online.

six

It was really a battle of who'd get my attention, my computers or my girlfriend. For the most part, computers won.

"LET'S DO THIS AGAIN. This time drums, guitar, vocals—come in at the end of Colin's intro."

Colin started again, running his fingers across the keyboard in a soft melody. As the drums began, he nodded his head to the rhythm and played off of the intricacies of the guitar lick.

The vocals came in. When they sang "I will open up my heart and let the healer set me free," Colin closed his eyes and thought about the words. *What's it like to open up your heart like that? God, can you really be my healer?* Colin felt the flicker of a longing inside.

"OK, that sounds good." The worship leader stepped away from the stage area. That was the cue for them to wrap up their practice. They'd return to the stage after the announcements from the youth pastor and after the icebreaker.

> **What's it like to open up your heart like that?**
> **God, can you really be my healer?**
> **Colin felt the flicker of a longing inside.**
>
> http://

Colin had been involved with the worship band for a few months. Playing helped him feel connected to God, at least in some ways. He enjoyed that part of youth group, but walking through the door into that crowd every week still left him gripped with tension and feeling like he'd rather be somewhere else.

He checked the connections for the speakers, then headed to a chair at the back corner of the room where he could have a good vantage point with minimal interaction.

Nique wasn't there yet. It made a huge difference when she was. He'd known her through church since he was in fourth grade, but they hadn't started talking until more recently. He'd told someone he liked her and then later heard she liked him too. So they started hanging out together more, sometimes going to movies with friends, chatting online, or talking on the phone. As he thought about her, a wave of excitement rippled through him.

The room was gradually filling as the group of teenagers, about ninety students, trickled in. There were almost too many to fit. Colin crossed his arms, slid down in his chair, and stretched out his legs. He watched as different ones arrived, found their friends, and then sat in groups or stood in different parts of the room—just hanging out. Some, coming straight from a job or sports, were in the back grabbing something to eat at the snack shack, Boarders.

Colin's attention shifted toward the stage where Mike, his youth pastor, was setting up a line of four chairs. Colin guessed it was for another of Mike's icebreaker games. He wondered what it would be this time. *One thing for sure—I won't be up there in one of those chairs. No way.*

EYES ONLINE : EYES ON LIFE

A soft touch of hands came down on his shoulders from behind. "Come on—come sit with us." It was Nique.

Colin felt the clash of emotions. He was glad to see her, wanted to be with her, but not sure he wanted to move from where he was. "I'm alright here. I—"

A soft touch of hands came down on his shoulders from behind. "Come on—come sit with us."

Nique came around to his side and grabbed his hand. "You're coming. We want you to sit with us."

He hesitated, but she kept pulling. Her warm smile was enough to persuade him. He'd do it for her. He smiled. "OK."

She laughed. "Come on, let's go." Then she pulled him until he stood.

They moved toward her circle of friends. Once there, he stayed a few steps away and listened to their talk about school and the youth group activities coming up.

"Let's get started." Mike held the microphone in his hand, ready to open the meeting. The stage lights highlighted his tall, thin frame and shone on his dark brown hair. He paced the stage while he waited.

Clusters of students began to break up and find seats. Colin sat down in a chair at the end of the row. Nique's friends laughed and slid back and forth to different seats. When everyone had finally settled on chairs, Nique ended up a couple of seats away from Colin. He glanced her way and watched her lean over and whisper to a friend. So different from him, she was animated and comfortable with the group. He was bummed she didn't sit next to him, but he definitely didn't mind being at the end, close to the wall.

The announcement video started. Colin liked those. In this clip, one of the teens read a children's book. Headshots of the youth leaders had been glued onto pictures in the book, and the announcements were written onto the pages. Everyone laughed.

> **So different from him, she was animated and comfortable with the group.**

Mike gave more details of the upcoming events and then transitioned into the icebreaker. He scanned the room. "I need four volunteers." Hands shot up.

Colin crossed his arms tighter and watched. Now that the group had grown, his pastor didn't do as many group activities, so Colin found it easier to avoid involvement. He'd keep his participation to the worship band—that was it.

The volunteers sat in the chairs on the stage and followed the instructions to take off their shoes. They were each handed a banana and told to peel it with their feet—fastest one wins free food from the snack shack.

The group roared and stomped their feet as they watched

the four race to maneuver their bananas into position to get them peeled. Colin shook his head. *So glad I'm not up there.*

Over the next few weeks, Colin and Nique grew closer and talked more and more. When they weren't at youth group, they connected on the phone or at least e-mailed or chatted online every day. He enjoyed that . . . most of the time . . .

Colin sat in front of his computer chatting with his East Coast friends, Mike and Steve, and also Kelly from the Midwest—friends he only knew online. Between comments, he had a couple of low-key online games going. One was a simple game where objects appeared and players attempted to blow up as many as possible. A chat box from Nique popped up.

> **Nique:** hi Colin
> **Colin:** hey Nique
> **Nique:** watcha doing?
> **Colin:** brb

Colin clicked to knock off the last few objects in one game, then closed that one and made a move in a game of chess he was playing against an online opponent.

> **He did want to see her. The bar flashed again.**
> ***And* he wanted to beat the game.**

> **Colin:** i'm back.
> **Nique:** so you want to do something
> **Nique:** come over?

While she typed, he had switched to type a quick response to Mike, then to Kelly. Then he read Nique's question. Did he want go anywhere right now? Yeah, he kinda did, but she lived on the other side of town and transportation was always a problem. A box on his task bar flashed. It was his turn to make a move in the chess game. *I could beat this guy this time . . .*

Nique: Colin?

He did want to see her. The bar flashed again. *And* he wanted to beat the game.

Colin: umm . . . no i can't. can't get a ride over right now.

He honestly couldn't, but his interest in Nique and his online activities constantly played tug-of-war with his attention. He kept juggling them, and he didn't like when the two were in direct competition. When so, the Internet often won.

A few months later, Colin walked through the fellowship hall after he'd set up and practiced for worship. He worked his way across the room to where Nique and her friends were hanging out. They were now dating, officially boyfriend-girlfriend. He really liked her—a lot. They were growing close.

> **She was beginning to convince him that not only did she care about him but others did too.**

One of the guys in the group greeted him as he walked by. "Hey, Colin."

He smiled and lifted his head in a nod. "Hey."

A few more steps and someone else turned from a conversation as Colin walked by. "Cool worship time last week."

"Yeah, it wasn't bad." Colin smiled again. He got to the other side of the room, where Nique stood. Dropping down onto a chair nearby, he stretched his arm across the back of the empty chair next to him and listened in on their conversation.

He watched Nique's excited explanation of a recent shopping trip and a crazy clerk who messed up the sale. She was so full of energy. He smiled. She was beginning to convince him that not only did she care about him but others did too. Her outgoing determination had helped him feel a little more comfortable at church.

What she thought about him mattered a lot—like not wanting him to cuss. He mostly left his word choices unchecked only with his school friends. But lately even they had started to notice that Colin was making progress in cleaning up his language.

Colin smiled to himself. Giving up cussing was one small change he'd chosen to make. It seemed to be making a difference in his relationship with God too. He felt encouraged, but there were still plenty of other areas of his life where he kept God at a distance. Like visiting the porn sites. He was beginning to get that it wasn't just a normal guy thing, and it wasn't so cool. He'd overheard Nique and some of her friends talking about what they liked and didn't like in guys. Looking at naked girls was in the didn't-like category. *So maybe God cares about that stuff too?* Colin felt a stab of guilt, but he fought to push the feeling away.

Nique's laughter pulled his attention back.

Colin coughed and shifted in his chair. *Not that big of a deal anyway. Besides, no one would know.*

At home that night he was back online, opening windows and traveling into the Internet's dark alleys. Even when he didn't visit porn sites every night, the pictures and seductive fantasies were tenaciously holding onto his heart and mind. Away from the computer, his thoughts were traveling the same back alleys. Images not only flashed through his mind, the desire for more toyed with his will to break free . . .

Did he want to? He wasn't sure.

> Turn my eyes from worthless things,
> and give me life through your word.
> Reassure me of your promise,
> which is for those who honor you.
> Help me abandon my shameful ways;
> your laws are all I want in life.
>
> PSALM 119:37-39 (*NLT*)

SMALL CHANGES

What would win out in getting Colin's attention? The life and the people he was beginning to connect with or his continued obsessions with the Internet? He was sensing that his life might not be matching up with what God or others who cared about him wanted for him. He even felt like he might want some of those things for himself, but it was hard. He said, "I began to have the desire to change, but I didn't have the strength of will to act on it." Colin needed to discover a strength beyond his own—God's.

Still, small changes were happening. By tenth grade, he was joining in more with the youth group, starting to be OK with being there. "I don't think I realized the situation with Nique helped until I was out of my shell," he remembered. In many ways, being around her pushed him toward being a little more connected. "She was a very social person, so spending time with her involved spending time with others."

Of his relationship with Nique, Colin said, "While she helped me get out of my shell, that didn't help me grow closer to God. The only reason I now wanted to go to youth group was to see her. Almost no other aspect of my life had changed."

Except his effort to clean up his language. Colin knows it's true that at first he only did that for Nique—girls were a strong motivator for him—but then that choice made a deeper difference. He said, "Looking back on it, that moment when I decided to stop cussing was pretty pivotal. It sounds weird, but it was the first time I let God take control. I knew cussing was a bad thing and by doing it, I was rebelling. So when I made the conscious effort to stop, it really started to transform my heart."

Small changes can lead to bigger ones. Somewhere in the fray of all that tumbled through Colin's mind, God was speaking and inviting him to something higher and better. His power was greater than what had sunk its claws into Colin's life and controlled his thoughts for far too long. If only Colin could begin to know that and to hear that voice above the loud confusion of his online obsessions.

The solitary nature of online activities makes it easy to spend hours doing things no one will ever know about. Talk with the teens and young adults you know about what would work for each of them to create accountability and foster responsible online use. Check in often with those whose struggles seem to be more intense.

Beginning to Listen

It doesn't matter how seemingly mild or hardcore our online activities and choices are—if they've got a hold on us, it's not easy to shake them, even with our good intentions and best efforts. It can be a struggle to follow through with what we know is best for us or what God is calling us to.

Katy, who said she spends too much time chatting online, has been fully aware of those moments she felt God prompting her. She admitted she hasn't always listened: "I've gotten pretty good at blocking him—not too much but enough where I'll ignore his call." But she knows that listening will make a difference. She said, "Now I think God wants me to try my best to overcome my overuse of online time. If I start overcoming this and sacrificing a few things, I'll spend more time with him and build that relationship more than any other online."

Sometimes we struggle with making our commitments consistent. We intend to do better but then let them slide.

Tiffany saw how she could become consumed by checking her Facebook profile; she began to make efforts to watch her time. She said, "I always do mean it when I want to change and spend less time online, but since it means limiting activities I enjoy doing online, it is, in a way, halfhearted." Her personal relationship with God became her motivator: "Christ calls us to a higher standard of behavior, so it helps me be motivated to be more responsible about spending time online."

And even when we *know* God is calling us toward change and a different focus or balance, it's still a journey to get to that place where we've conquered the pull we've felt.

For Marius, who lives in South Africa, competitive online gaming became a major focus in his life, even to the point that by age nineteen, he spent most weekday evenings and entire weekends playing against friends and other groups. "God started to show me how meaningless it all was—how pursuing gaming had no true fulfillment, that this would ultimately destroy me, and that God had abundant life for me."

His decision didn't go over well with those he played with: "I told my co-clan leader that I had given my life to Jesus and that I was going to stop playing games and follow Jesus. He took it really badly because we were on the verge of being one of the top clans in our country. He couldn't understand why I would give it all up for God."

Marius made a lot of determined changes. "I went to church regularly, met a great group of Christian friends at the church, spent time in God's Word every day, prayed every day, and was growing as a Christian. I learned how to play the drums and was in the worship team at church. I met my wife at that same church."

Not too long after he married, he experienced some personal struggles and decided he needed a hobby. He bought a new PC and a few games and was right back where he started. "I would quickly read a chapter of the Bible with my wife around 9 PM, give her a kiss good-night, then rush to the study to play Guild Wars."

Marius's wife let it go and didn't say anything, and he kept it up. He thought it was working well. Those who knew him wouldn't have guessed anything different. "Most would look at me and not see someone who would be addicted to anything. I was healthy, had a happy marriage, and a good job."

Marius thought he had it all figured out, but it hadn't yet sunk in that the hundreds of hours he spent gaming was taking a toll, especially on his closest relationships—with his wife and with God. He said, "I still loved God and spoke with him, but he wasn't first in my life at all."

Marius had an enormous capacity to dedicate time, energy, and focus toward something he cared about. Most of us do. But do we see the battle? Do we see the pull toward empty, even destructive activities? God wants the best for us. His power, greater than anything and anyone, can break us free and help us get our eyes focused back on life. Just ask him.

Invite the teens you know to join you in a challenge to stay off the computer for one week—for anything except essential tasks like homework. Next time you meet, talk about what was easy and what was hard. Discuss strategies for a balanced use of online time as all of you head into a new week.

We set up our game play. We know who we are, what our mission is, and we settle in to fight hard and make it to the end victorious. It's a mind-set of success.

That kind of mind-set could work for your journey out of Internet obsessions too.

First, a mind-set of success involves a daily keeping in mind of who we are in a relationship with God and, ultimately, where we're headed for eternity. Colossians 3:1-3 says, "Since, then, you have been raised with Christ, set your hearts on things above, where Christ is seated at the right hand of God. Set your minds on things above, not on earthly things. For you died, and your life is now hidden with Christ in God." When you are one of God's own, you can ask him to help you grab hold of the depth of that relationship and identity and what it means for your life now *and* for eternity.

Verse 5 of that same passage in Colossians adds that we are to cut out of our lives anything that keeps us from that mind-set: "Put to death, therefore, whatever belongs to your earthly nature: sexual immorality, impurity, lust, evil desires and greed, which is idolatry."

So a second part of the mind-set of success involves intentionally focusing on living in a way we know honors God. "Those who live according to the sinful nature have their minds set on what that nature desires; but those who live in accordance with the Spirit have their minds set on what the Spirit desires" (Romans 8:5). Verse 6, as paraphrased in *The Message*, describes where this view takes us: "Obsession with self in these matters is a dead end; attention to God leads us out into the open, into a spacious, free life." Amazing!—if we can just apply that to online choices. It creates quite a picture of our options—a dead-end life or wide-open freedom.

Still heading for that victory, a third part of the mind-set of success focuses on an attitude of humility toward God as he begins to make changes in our lives. Look at what he told Daniel, a young Jewish prophet and captive of Babylon: "Do not be afraid, Daniel. Since the first day that you set your mind to gain understanding and to humble yourself before God, your words were heard, and I have come in response to them" (Daniel 10:12).

Those words apply to us. As we are completely honest before God, fully willing to admit our mess-ups and weaknesses—but also to set our mind toward gaining understanding and freedom—our journey will be set toward victory. With God we can do it.

God, you ask for wholehearted commitment toward you, which also goes for the choices I make online and how I plan to move toward using that time in the way that best honors you. Even when I fully get that, I can start out determined to make changes, then slide into halfhearted attempts that eventually take me right back where I was before. Help me keep my focus fully set toward seeking what pleases you and ultimately brings me to the freedom you want for me. AMEN.

> **My son, give me your heart**
> **and let your eyes keep to my ways.**
> PROVERBS 23:26

GOING DEEPER

■ Maybe some people in your life have a different impression than you of how you're *really* doing with your online choices. What are the benefits that come from being totally up front? What steps can you take to be just that?

■ Have you tried to set goals to balance or quit an online activity, then let those goals slide after a while? How can you bring God into the picture to help you tackle those with a greater sense of intentionality and focus? Get with someone you can trust—a parent, your pastor, a mentor—and ask them for specific ways you can do this. Ask them to be your friend through this, to provide accountability.

■ Look at the three mind-sets listed at the end of this chapter—grabbing hold of your identity as one of God's own, having an intentional focus on what honors God, and having an attitude of humility as God makes changes in your life. List how each can impact your online choices this week.

DEEPER STILL

Step outside and find a quiet place where you can see the immenseness of the sky—either in daylight or by moonlight. Be as still as you can and think of God. Ask him to show you a picture of the spacious freedom he wants you to live out. After some moments of quiet, write a prayer letter to God, asking him to help you keep your mind-set toward that freedom he showed you.

seven

I had an experience. I was surrounded by Christians all worshiping, all praying. Then I came home and it was like "That was nice. Now back to school and my life."

COLIN SAT A COUPLE OF STEPS UP A STAIRCASE from most of the others, leaned his elbows back on the step behind him, and scanned the room. He and thirty others from the youth group were scattered across a large open room on the lower floor of the Gold Rush Lodge. The rustic building was clustered among other lodges and small cabins on a sprawling conference ground in the Sierra Mountains. The church reserved the cabin every February for its winter youth retreat.

The lights dimmed, and a video projector lit up a wall in the far corner. Conversations lowered to whispers as everyone settled into watching *Remember the Titans*. Colin had seen it before. He guessed his youth pastor planned to use it for the retreat to hit on some challenging lessons.

> **He found himself rooting for those who were misunderstood.**
> *Just give him a chance.*

Nique sat on the step next to him. Other friends were nearby on other steps, on the floor, or in chairs. Colin shifted and smiled. This year his comfort level was up a couple of notches from the year before. He'd come his freshman year because it was something he was given a choice about, and he thought it would be fun. But once there, he felt out of place and awkward, and wished he hadn't come.

This time, he couldn't say he was completely at ease, but having friends to hang out with made a difference. And he had Nique. She had really pushed him to go this year.

Colin watched the football players on screen battle out their racial prejudices. He didn't think too deeply about it, mostly just watched, but once in a while he felt a twinge of familiarity as the guys judged someone else without really knowing that person. He found himself rooting for those who were misunderstood. *Just give him a chance.*

More of those in his youth group were giving him that chance. As he looked out across the room toward the screen, he spotted different ones that he now knew better than he did a year ago. He had begun to feel a part of what was going on at youth group, started to have friends—real friends who cared about him.

He glanced over at Nique. She was totally into the movie. He smiled. She had a huge part in the good stuff that had happened. He was stubborn, but she was too. She wouldn't let him get by with sitting on the sidelines.

Colin bent one leg up, dropped his elbow to his thigh, and propped his head in his hand. He noticed Mike sitting off to the side. He thought about how his oldest brother had a made a great connection with this pastor. Not surprising. Mike was caring, solid in his teaching, and great with teens. And it was a guarantee his retreats would be packed with meaning. Colin looked forward to seeing what was coming this weekend.

> **As lonely as it felt, he didn't mind being different. He respected himself . . . well, mostly.**

He turned his attention back to the movie. The coaches were struggling to get the black and white team members to work things through. "I don't care if you like each other. You *will* respect each other," one of the coaches was saying.

Respect. Even with all he had faced with being ridiculed and struggling to fit in, Colin felt like he respected others—a lot. And as lonely as it felt, he didn't mind being different. He respected himself . . . well, mostly. His thoughts shifted to parts of his life where he knew he still messed up. *I know I'm not doing everything like I should.* He really didn't read the Bible much. He made choices that he knew weren't good for him. It frustrated him that at times he didn't care.

The movie played on. Gary, a big, burly white guy, had been in a car accident and was paralyzed, but by this time in the movie, he and Julius—a big, burly black guy—had overcome huge hurdles to form a strong friendship. Gary and Julius were talking:

Gary: "I was afraid of you, Julius. I was only hating my brother."

Julius: "When all this is over, you and I are going to move into the same neighborhood together."

seven

The movie ended with the toughest football game the team had played—the state championship against an undefeated team. True story, and Colin knew the ending. The Titans would win.

> **Chris—he was the target of more prejudices and misunderstandings than Colin would ever experience anywhere. Being different wasn't easy.**

The final scene concluded and as the credits rolled, the lights came on. Mike stood. "The Titans had some pretty tough obstacles to overcome. It took a team effort to achieve all they did—and they had a lot more to shoot for than just winning some games." He walked a few steps across the front, one hand rubbing his jaw. When he stopped, he turned to them. His voice was earnest. "It takes a lot of strength to put aside differences to work toward a common call."

Colin thought about that. He tried not to focus on the differences in others, though he was sharply aware of his own. *And* those of his brother Chris—the target of more prejudices and misunderstandings than Colin would ever experience anywhere. Being different wasn't easy.

I want to get involved more, but can others accept me the way I am? Even with the progress he'd made, he wasn't yet sure of that.

Over the next half hour, Mike highlighted movie scenes to challenge the students to leadership and unity. Colin listened.

He looked around the room and spotted some of the juniors and seniors who were really involved. *True leaders. That's who Mike is talking about. Something I'll never be.*

The next night, low tables were set up with bowls of grapes and pieces of bread. The room was lit by candles. Instrumental worship music played in the background. Everyone was quiet and deep in thought, and they were instructed to recline at the tables in the same way Jesus might have done with his disciples.

Mike led the group through a service of remembrance of Jesus' last meal with the disciples, and of his death and resurrection—Communion in a way that Colin had never experienced before. He guessed none of them had. It almost felt like they were there in Galilee with Jesus, looking into his eyes as he offered the bread and the wine.

> **He'd been at this point in the past, only to see everything slide right back to the way it was before.**

Scriptures were read and Colin thought about Jesus on the last night, loving and serving the disciples who had become his friends. The Son of God. Jesus knew he was going to give his life for them. The meal represented God's covenant with his followers—that Jesus would be giving up his life, shedding his blood for the forgiveness of their sins.

For everyone's sins. Even mine.

Colin felt the impact of the moment deep inside. Emotions stirred and a challenge grabbed hold of his heart. Could he make the changes needed? Could he be different?

I want to, God.

Later, as Colin crawled onto his bunk, he still sensed the closeness to God he'd felt earlier. He wanted the feeling to stay with him. He'd been at this point in the past, only to see everything slide right back to the way it was before.

This time it will be different.

At school the next week, Colin sat with TJ, a guy he'd talked to a few times in his social studies class. *Maybe I could talk to him about . . .* He hesitated, then felt the courage rise and decided he'd go for it before he lost his nerve.

"Hey, I was just wondering if you ever had any questions about God."

"I don't know. What do you mean?

OK, this isn't so easy. "You know. About who God is. About being a Christian."

"No, not really."

"Oh, OK."

TJ shrugged and turned his attention back to his book.

Colin wondered how he could end the awkwardness but still leave things open for TJ to talk to him another time. "Uh . . ."

TJ looked up at him again.

Colin wasn't sure what to say next but knew he needed to say something. He blurted, "You know, if you have questions, just ask—anytime. I'll do what I can to find the answers."

"Yeah, alright. Thanks." His friend grinned and went back to his reading.

That was it. Colin was excited that he might have another talk with TJ. He could tell him more about Jesus, even invite him to church.

But as the weeks passed, there were no more conversations like that—with TJ or anyone else. Colin began to lose the closeness to God he had felt at the retreat. The feelings were slipping away, and he didn't know how to keep them going. It was too hard. His determination wavered. Sadness, with its familiar inky fog, began to shroud the hope he had felt. His real life and online choices continued to reflect a mixed commitment.

He tried to convince himself it was OK.

> It was too hard. His determination wavered. Sadness, with its familiar inky fog, began to shroud the hope he had felt.
>
> http://

Online at home, he settled into what had grown to feel comfortable—withdrawing from activities and people, escaping. Feeling the weight of his weariness, he added a comment on a forum and found his friend Steve online. A site they both visited often was a place where they could choose hand-drawn emoticons representing their moods. Colin inserted a scribble with a combination of a confused and a sad face.

"not happy i take it?" Steve typed.

"no." Colin thought about why, then entered more text. He told him about the retreat, how he wanted to do better with his relationship with God but didn't know how. Neither said much more about that, but the chat continued as they joined others in a dialogue about emoticons they were trying on their blogs.

> **He felt a twinge deep in his chest,**
> **an ache that he didn't know how to fill.**
> *I don't know how to do this life stuff, God.*
> *I don't know if I want to.*

Just as he had been doing at the youth group, Colin was gradually making a few good online friends who cared about trying to live out their faith in Christ. He thought about that. They struggled and questioned like he did, but they didn't know everything about him. They didn't know the depths his sadness could reach, how hard he fought to find his place in his home or school or youth group, how far he'd go to push his loneliness away. He thought about the porn, how he turned to it more often, how it was consuming his thoughts in ways he never imagined. *They can't find out about that. No one can.*

He felt a twinge deep in his chest, an ache that he didn't know how to fill. *I don't know how to do this life stuff, God. I don't know if I want to.*

> He has rescued us from the dominion of darkness and
> brought us into the kingdom of the Son he loves,
> in whom we have redemption, the forgiveness of sins.
> COLOSSIANS 1:13, 14

It isn't always a plan. Sometimes it just happens: living out what feels comfortable—what's accepted—even if it is role-playing and no one knows who you really are. The walls are up. It's called survival. The problem is that often while we're keeping everyone at a distance and making sure they don't find out everything about who we are, we lose track of who we can become.

In most ways, Colin was doing his best to be himself. But he still only let his friends see the parts he wanted them to—at youth group, at school, or online. Each group saw some different sides that others didn't, whether it was an evident faith in Christ or just being one of the guys he was around at the time.

The retreat had seemed to be that one opportunity when maybe he'd grab hold of something that would make a difference and become a part of him—no matter who was around. But for the second year in a row, he found that the retreat experience didn't seem to stick. Looking back, he said, "It's a Christian-saturated environment. You're in your Bible the whole time, surrounded by Christians. You get back to the rest of the world, and you realize that kind of person isn't accepted."

Colin did genuinely want to be who he thought God wanted him to be. It just wasn't happening. "I never felt like I was faking it, but I hadn't figured out that I needed God to make this work. And I didn't try anything different. I just went back to the way things were before." That included his online activities. Though connecting more with friends in the youth group was helping, hours of time online hadn't changed much yet, and his habit of viewing porn continued to be a secret he kept from everyone.

Still, his youth pastor saw the beginnings of some changes. He'd known Colin through those years when he stayed to himself. Now in Colin's second year of high school, he seemed to want to be there. Mike said, "It was like night and day. By this time he walked in the room and he might have half a dozen people saying, 'Hey Colin,' where in sixth grade, no one was going to notice him. And he didn't want them to."

At this time, the older core leaders in the youth group—including Colin's oldest and outgoing brother—were moving on to other things. But Mike already saw another younger core that he felt would be setting the tone and defining the group. Colin was a part of that mix.

Mike said, "The interesting thing was, any one of those kids, if they walked into the room, would be the most unlikely . . . almost, a wallflower-type kid. They would have very little influence on their own during that time. Their strength really was that they awkwardly came together, and it was like, 'OK, we kind of work together. This is good.'"

About Colin specifically, Mike remembered, "You could see him slowly but surely taking his place and sensing he had some relevance. And that's when you saw him every so often say something like, 'Wow, God's really saying this to me,' or he'd make some kind of comment like, 'Hey, I'm really trying to invite this friend from school to youth group.' You could see him taking an active role in his own faith. Maybe trying to reach out to people around him and in the group, kind of being a leader, unofficially, at that point."

Colin didn't see himself that way. Yes, he was beginning to want to be there and he was finding a place in the group, but he didn't view himself as a potential leader—at all. He was still trying to figure out where his faith in God fit into the picture. So far he had discovered you couldn't just drop God into your life any way or at any time you wanted and make it work.

Colin was far from done with his journey and wouldn't have guessed what was around the next bend. Soon he wouldn't be able to hide his secret struggles any longer.

Realize it's tough for many teens to feel comfortable with who they are—whether or not they seem to be fitting in. Watch for opportunities to compliment others and encourage character qualities—like kindness and generosity—and be willing and available to meet needs.

A ROLE TO PLAY

RPGs (role-playing games) offer an opportunity for players to be who they want to be. For porn sites, the visitor secretly steps into another role, allowing unchecked fantasies. Even networking sites and chats are crammed with interactions where people aren't fully honest about themselves. Roles are played there too, as appearances, abilities, and experiences are switched up depending on what seems, at the moment, to sound more interesting or acceptable. The person who may be shy and timid in real life can become someone entirely different online.

For some it means being who they feel they are but without the fear of rejection. Tyler noticed this. He said, "People are more bold online. They're more willing to put themselves out there than they are in real life because if they get rejected it's not that big of a deal—just turn the computer off or whatever."

Tiffany said that online she is "maybe more fun—less serious and more spazzy." She also said, "It's not that I try to be this way—it just happens. And it bugs me when I realize what's going on. But in a way, I feel like this happens to everybody. We're kind of used to each other's online personalities versus our personalities in real life." Her observation: it's often accepted and almost expected to have a different or bolder online persona.

But some take it a few steps beyond bold and take risks they never would want to in real life. Katy sees a big change when she goes online: "As soon as I log in—I feel like I'm a different person. Like when a guy gets on and starts chatting with me, I act different. Flirty mostly. Too bubbly, over-excited maybe." She feels that being online and going into chat rooms nearly transforms her into another person. She said, "When some guy starts a conversation with me, I like that he is talking to me, so I indulge him. Ask my friends. When I get around my real guy friends, I don't act like this at all."

Take this just one step further—and you're a completely different person.

Ryan said that online he could get rid of all his insecurities and be whoever he wanted to be. "When I was overweight, I could be six-foot-two. I could be the quarterback on the football team if I wanted." But he knows such efforts only temporarily obscure reality. "You could be confident online, but you're really not. To others, you're still overweight, still have these insecurities, and are still self-conscious."

Tom Neven, editorial director for Focus on the Family's Youth Outreach, believes that "a lack of meaningful relationships at home or school" is a big contributor to misusing the Internet. And, "It's easy to get lost in chat rooms where you don't have to be your real self."

Walt Mueller, author and the founder of the Center for Parent and Youth Understanding—which studies youth culture and marketing and its rapid changes—sees the Internet's natural interactive environment as a place for youth to create and communicate. He also sees its role, as a part of media, in "answering questions, shaping worldview, determining how they will live the rest of their lives." And the flip side? He added, "This is just normal life for them—the way 'it's supposed to be'—but they are more lonely and broken."

Lonely. Once we close our networking site or click out of a chat or game, we're still who we are. Hurting, depressed, feeling insecure, wanting a parent or just one friend to show us they care, wishing just once that someone would see beyond our blemishes to our potential.

Sure there are opportunities online, but no amount of online connections can help you feel more comfortable in the skin you live in . . . or in the world that is outside your room or front door.

> Work at doing your part in creating an environment of acceptance in your home, community, or youth group. Get the teens and young adults you're working with to start talking about whether they feel accepted or not. Encourage responses that help those who are there feel comfortable being who they are, and comfortable growing into all they can become for God.

YOU—REAL

What we do online doesn't stay online. In a huge way, when we step away from the computer, how we were and what we did there goes right along with us into our real-world activities and relationships. Images and experiences remain. They impact us and shape us—for good or bad. That goes for the roles we've played, whether in a game, in a chat, on a networking site, or at a porn site.

You know. You've felt it.

And if you're role-playing with others, there's a good chance you're doing that with God—the one who, guaranteed, has the highest expectations of who you should be. They are high, but for a good reason. They're filled with the deepest love and the highest hopes for you. But God wants the *real* you, not the person you think you should be when you're with him.

Outside a town in Samaria, Jesus met a woman at a well who tried to give a different impression of who she was. She was intelligent, maybe once beautiful, but she had thrown away many years of her life through choices that left her used up, poor, and weary. Still, she was determined to keep up the facade with this Jewish man at the well.

Jesus, being God in the flesh, knew she would be there. He knew all about her, but especially her need for "living water"—God's mercy that would quench the thirst of her soul. She was skeptical and challenged Jesus. He asked her to go get her husband, knowing this request would lead to the truth.

She responded, "I have no husband" (John 4:17). And Jesus said, "You are right when you say you have no husband. The fact is, you have had five husbands, and the man you now have is not your husband" (vv. 17, 18).

At this point, she hadn't figured out she was talking to God in the flesh, but she did realize she couldn't hide who she was from this man. From here, Jesus challenged the woman toward complete truth and realness. He said, "But the time is coming—it has, in fact, come—when what you're called will not matter and where you go to worship will not matter. It's *who you are* and the *way you live* that count before God. Your worship must engage your spirit in the pursuit of truth. That's the kind of people the Father is out looking for: those who are simply and honestly themselves before him in their worship" (v. 23, *The Message*, emphasis added).

The story goes on to emphasize the importance of coming to God without even a hint of pretense. Verse 24 says, "Those who worship him must do it out of their very being, their spirits, their true selves, in adoration" (*The Message*).

No role-playing needed. Fully, honestly, the real you—that's who God wants a deep relationship with. And that's who he hopes you can grow comfortable being with everyone else.

God, I don't need to hide anything from you. You know me with all of my blemishes and shortcomings, and you love me and want the very best for me. Help me connect with you in truthfulness. Make my life an expression of that honesty in every area, online and off. And when I'm tempted to put on a role out of fear or loneliness, remind me of who I am and who I am becoming in you. Show me how I can make deeper and real connections with the people you've put in my life. AMEN.

> But you, dear friends, must build each other up in your most holy faith, pray in the power of the Holy Spirit, and await the mercy of our Lord Jesus Christ, who will bring you eternal life. In this way, you will keep yourselves safe in God's love.
>
> JUDE 20, 21 (*NLT*)

GOING DEEPER

■ Where do you see yourself acting different than who you really are—in real life or online? What might you be hoping to gain or to avoid by acting differently than you normally would?

■ Some people role-play because they fear rejection, are tired of being ignored, or feel pressure to fit in and belong. Or there might be other reasons. Think about a time you tried to be someone different than who you really are. What was going on that made you want to do that?

■ Do you have secrets about your online activities that are preventing you from growing close to God? What are you learning about God's love for you—and his knowledge of your life—that can help you come to him fully honest about all areas of your life?

DEEPER STILL

List all the strengths you have.

- Your character: Are you helpful, generous, dependable?

- Your gifts: Are you artistic, musical, athletic, techie?

- Your abilities: Can you build things, figure out problems easily, get creative in the kitchen?

Think beyond the suggestions given.

Now list ways that each of your strengths can be used to connect more deeply with others in your community or church. Think of specific people you can encourage or help, specific ministries and community locations where you can volunteer your time. Choose one or two for this week.

eight

I'm glad that I was honest, because if I hadn't been,
I might still be trapped in pornography.

COLIN CRUMPLED UP HIS LUNCH GARBAGE, tossed it in the trash can, and then walked the few steps through the door into the computer lab. He had some time to kill before the end of lunch period, so he pulled up a chair in front of one of the computers to play Warcraft. Four of the other guys he hung out with joined him and sat down at different computers around the room. One, Jacob, took the computer next to him.

Andrew, across the room, had the full-version and set up the game for all of them, activating computer players to make the game more unpredictable.

As Colin sat there waiting for the games to load on all the computers, he shot a quick glance at each of the guys. He realized he didn't really know most of them. Some were different friends than those he had hung out with the first two years of high school. When all of them ate together at lunch, they talked about their common interests—computers and gaming. The few times they got together outside of school, they played video games at one of their houses. Not too much conversation. Just games.

Colin thought about that. *What are their lives like outside of school or when we aren't all playing computer or video games together? Do they have jobs? Who are their* real *friends? What are their families like?*

He didn't ask out loud. Knew he never would. Knew they wouldn't either. It was almost as if the other parts of their lives were unreal. They were more into how they related within the computer world—and games like the one they were about to play.

The game finished loading, and they picked up where they'd left off the last time, Colin human rather than orc. With their towers and bases built up, their soldiers and units in place, and their well-worked strategies, they moved across the terrain, ready to take each other down.

> It was almost as if the other parts of their lives were unreal. They were more into how they related within the computer world—and games like the one they were about to play.

Colin and Jacob had a pact. They wouldn't attack each other. The game started, and they each concentrated on keying the moves. Though in the same room, they entered text in a chat box to communicate. Colin had his sound muted, but he could hear the nature and battle sound effects coming from the other computers.

For the next forty-five minutes they were at war, gathering resources, building up their forces, defending or losing their territory. A bell rang, warning them the lunch period was about to end—ten minutes to the next bell.

"Almost time to go," Andrew said from across the room.

They squeezed in five more minutes of game time.

Colin quickly maneuvered his men into a strategic place before he stopped. He'd want to be in a good position to begin next time they played. He glanced up at the clock. He wasn't worried about being late. Today he didn't have a class after the lunch period, so he planned on hanging out with Nique at a lunch place near her school—it was one way to see her, their schools being closer to each other than their houses were. To trim the twenty-minute trip in half, he'd use his skateboard, but he knew he'd better hurry if he was going to make it on time.

After he got home that day, Colin posted on his blog and visited the profiles of his online friends—especially Mike's and Steve's. Since they lived on the opposite coast, he'd never met them, but those two plus his friend Kelly were becoming pretty good Internet friends for him. They all got very honest in their chats or blogs, knew when anyone was stoked about something happening, or when one was feeling really down. They left comments on the blog sites to encourage each other and chatted on AIM quite a bit.

> **The next question got really personal.**
> *Do you look at porn?*

Colin clicked on Mike's AIM profile. The side column had an image link to a "crush calculator." If you entered names of three people of the opposite sex you had a crush on, it would determine which one was most suited for you. Colin had tried these things before. He clicked on it, just for fun. Of course Nique's name would be the one that was selected.

eight

A survey popped up. Colin scanned the few first questions. Not too bad.

He shrugged. *No one will see the answers anyway.*

One by one, he answered them: *First name? Age? Who do you have crush on?* Then Colin stopped. The next question got really personal.

Do you look at porn? Colin didn't know if he should answer that one. Finally he did. *Yes.*

How many times a day? Colin hesitated again, then typed in "more than i should." And the questions got more personal from there, asking about other sexual habits. Colin answered them all.

At the bottom of the survey was a button to click. He was curious about what the survey would show and certain that no one would see the results anyway. He clicked to submit the survey.

A message flashed: *You've been fooled. Your survey has been sent to Mike.*

"Noooo!" Colin gripped the mouse. The screen went still. No way to get the survey back. Now someone would know. *What will Mike think of me now?*

A message flashed: *You've been fooled. Your survey has been sent to Mike.*

Colin stared at his computer monitor in shock. His stomach tightened and twisted. He got mad. Then madder. *How could Mike do that? Jerk.* In his head he began to compose a

EYES ONLINE : EYES ON LIFE

message. He opened his e-mail program, clicked on "new," and started typing.

```
Mike,
I took the survey on your profile.
DON'T open it or read it. Delete it.
Colin
```

He sent the message, pushed away from the computer, and got up to get something to eat. He couldn't believe it. *No one was supposed to find out. Now Mike knows.* It felt like a giant spotlight shone on his life and announced: "Dude—you're exposed. No hiding it now."

Mike: Colin, i've struggled with the same problem.
No way. Not Mike.

He went to the kitchen, couldn't think of anything he felt like eating. His stomach felt sick. He grabbed a Mountain Dew out of the fridge and headed back to his room.

He flipped the tab and waited. Took a sip. Waited some more.

An AIM chat box opened up. It was Mike.

```
Colin: did you read it?
Mike:  i got your e-mail after i'd already
       opened it.
```

Great. The cursor flashed. So did Colin's anger.

```
Mike:  sorry
```

Mike: Colin, i've struggled with the same problem

No way. Not Mike.

Colin: really?
Mike: yeah, since junior high
Mike: even trading floppies full of the stuff with friends
Colin: wow . . . no one knows about me. not any of my friends
Colin: until now

It helped that Mike could relate, but Colin was still mad. His jaw tightened. *Why did he leave the stupid survey on his site?* Mike's next comment gave an answer.

Mike: yeah, i know . . . sorry. i put up that link a while ago. it led to a different survey then.
Mike: man, i'm really sorry
Colin: i'll get over it

Yeah, someday. He knew he wouldn't stay mad, but right now? He couldn't believe he'd been tricked.

Mike: when my parents found out they threatened to ground me for life. i stopped for a while but figured out how to find it online without them knowing
Colin: what happened?
Mike: i finally decided I needed to do what I could to stop . . .

Colin saw the notation that Mike was still typing. He waited.

Mike: i prayed. I went to a site that had a program and accountability. they have bible verses that I memorize. that helped me a lot

Mike: maybe it's something you could try

Mike: they ask you to pick an accountability partner . . . if you want I could do that

Colin let the cursor flash again while he thought things through. Was he ready for that kind of step?

Mike: they ask you to pick an accountability partner . . . if you want I could do that

Colin drew in a breath and let it out slowly. Maybe it was time.

Colin: ok

Over the next few weeks Colin tried the program. Each day included several questions to answer about how you were doing. With his friend's accountability, he knew the commitment included doing the program even when he didn't feel like it. A lot of times he didn't. He had to answer honestly. It was hard. And it was getting boring. He knew all the verses. They seemed

eight

to be geared toward someone who had grown up without any Bible knowledge, and he had heard it all. He knew for himself it was more a matter of taking it to heart.

He wrote Mike and let him know he was dropping out.

"but i still need accountability," he typed to Mike.

"you've got it," Mike wrote back.

You were once darkness, but now you are light in the Lord. Live as children of light.

EPHESIANS 5:8

CAUGHT

So much for keeping his viewing of porn a secret. But some secrets aren't meant to stay hidden—especially when they're emotionally, physically, and spiritually destructive.

As many are when their secret is discovered, Colin had been angry at first—he'd felt betrayed—but as the months went by, he realized that if he hadn't honestly answered the survey and hit that submit button, he might still be caught in pornography.

He said, "I was afraid of everything coming to the light." Of this unintentional prank Colin says today, "It brought (my viewing of porn) out into the light, and while I don't broadcast it to everyone, I don't necessarily hide this sin."

Mike apologized "like apologizing was going out of style." He felt bad that it happened the way it did, but he also realized it became an important turning point for Colin. "There were several different questions that revealed a lot of things that he would not have wanted me to know. Somehow God was able to use that in a way that I never could have imagined."

In many ways, Colin was fortunate the survey went to someone who took it in a positive direction. "Confession time—I was going through the exact same conflict that he was going through," Mike said. So they became accountability partners for each other. Mike had already been through a Bible-based online program and recommended it.

Though Colin chose not to continue, he was glad he'd tried it. "It got me through this horribly dark spot in my life," he said. It also rooted deeply inside him "the value of accountability"—whether through friends, online programs, or strong filters. That would prove to be a key for Colin in the coming months and years as the lure of pornography would continue to tug at his mind.

About his general online use he said, "I was still semi-addicted to the Internet. I spent a majority of my time there, but now I wasn't so socially awkward. I talked with people more offline than I ever had before. I made lasting friendships at church—people I'm still friends with now." He had more battles ahead, but he had taken some great first steps.

Progress. God wasn't going to let Colin go until he was completely free.

Many support groups are available online, but consider offering face-to-face support to someone or starting a group that helps teens or young adults spend more time away from their computers. Include Bible study and prayer to help make those spiritual disciplines a part of their road to recovery. Invite pastors and professionals who can offer their leadership or expertise.

WAKE-UP CALLS

Sometimes it takes a shake-up for us to get to that place where we're willing to take an honest look at what we're doing online.

Katy admitted to chatting for long periods of time and constantly checking her profile and e-mail to see if she had any messages or posts—from guys especially. It felt great when one guy told her she was someone special. "I began to think I was the only girl he ever flirted with online and talked to me like he did. I really thought I was the only one." Her wake-up call came when she saw that he was doing the same thing with another girl. "It may seem like a small situation. In my heart it was huge."

Realizing how pulled in she got, Katy saw the importance of bringing God into her choices. She said, "The best way for God to be involved would be if we let him in and asked him for his help. Also, by accepting we have a problem, then we're opening our heart and humbling ourselves, and that's a good way for God to be in your choice to change."

Elize, a twenty-something, struggled with excessive shopping and gambling online. When she'd see something she wanted, she'd do nearly anything to get it. One time she got caught in a scam and lost a lot of money. Now she says, "I know with God's help I can stop. There are better things in life, and your life is so much richer by spending quality time with God."

God worked in Marius's life in yet another way. Consumed in his gaming world, he could think of little else. He once calculated he had played Guild Wars for eight hundred hours over an eleven-month period—not counting his other computer activities.

One night he realized he wasn't enjoying any of it. He began to feel God prompting him to stop gaming and start studying the Bible. His initial response: "I was not impressed with this idea at all. How could I give up gaming? I loved it." Then he realized, "Games had become my idol. I'd spend five minutes reading a chapter of the Bible, then spend three to four hours playing games."

Responding immediately to God moving in his life wasn't easy. "I still fought the feeling a little longer. It was a choice God had placed before me, but I felt him say that if I decided to chase after him, I had no idea how amazing it would be." So Marius got on his knees. "I asked for his forgiveness for placing those games before my relationship with him."

Johan, whose struggle has been pornography, believes strongly that we need to take the step to get on board with what God wants to do in our lives. He said, "God is central to our liberty in so many ways. I do believe, though, that the journey to freedom begins with a very honest conversation with him."

Stop and consider how you can get God involved in bringing you to that freedom Johan talks about. Start with that honest conversation.

> The person struggling with online obsessions may not know how to begin to have an honest conversation with God. Be willing to offer suggestions, pray with your friend, or help set up a solid mentoring situation for him or her.

ON TO GREATER THINGS

OK, so maybe a situation has happened that exposed your own online traps. You might have felt angry, scared, resistant—all kinds of emotions—and maybe anything but willing to go along with what God wants for you. You may even be tempted to fall for the old lie that God only wants to take the fun out of everything.

Not even close.

God isn't anti-Internet. He's just got a whole lot more in mind for your life—freedom from the traps, but also excitement, energy, and fullness beyond just your online existence.

Jesus said, "The thief comes only to steal and kill and destroy; I have come that they may have life, and have it to the full" (John 10:10). See the intent of those battling for your soul. Satan tries to rob and destroy, but Jesus comes to offer the opposite—a life filled up, overflowing with more than you can imagine.

That fullness begins by connecting to him in a relationship. Do you know that when he was tortured and nailed to the cross, and hung there bleeding and then dying, he had your secret traps in mind? As much as our culture may play it down, sin is ugly and real, and it separates every one of us from God: "All of us, like sheep, have strayed away. We have left God's paths to follow our own. Yet the Lord laid on him the sins of us all" (Isaiah 53:6, *NLT*). *All* our sins on Jesus. Wow.

Let that sink in, and then consider that through a relationship with Christ you are free from anything that has mastered you in the past. Look at what Romans 8:2 says about that: "And because you belong to him, the power of the life-giving Spirit has freed you from the power of sin that leads to death" (*NLT*). That's freedom, not just through God's forgiveness of the sin, but also freedom from the *power* that it has had on your life.

So let your online traps and secrets be brought out into the open—especially to God, but also to others who can help. Invite that deep connection to Jesus and the life-giving Spirit working in you, freeing you. You've got a great life ahead.

> *God, I want to be fully honest about my online struggles and obsessions. Help me to see their emptiness and the destructive ways they consume my thoughts and time. Work in me so I gain the understanding and the faith to pursue a deeper relationship with you and claim the fullness you desire for me. Show me clearly my great need for you and the freedom and rest I'll find in knowing you better.* AMEN.

> May you experience the love of Christ, though it is too great to understand fully. Then you will be made complete with all the fullness of life and power that comes from God.
>
> EPHESIANS 3:19 (*NLT*)

GOING DEEPER

■ Look at your online traps, especially those that few others (or none) know about. What feelings come to mind when you think about telling others or when you consider giving them up?

■ Sometimes we forget to look beyond what we're currently experiencing. What would a fuller life, free from any online traps—big or small—look like to you?

■ Have you had an honest conversation with God about what you do online? If you did that, if you were brutally honest, what would you tell him now?

DEEPER STILL

Here's another opportunity to get creative. Pull out a large sheet of paper and draw the outline of a person. Using some of the Scriptures and ideas from this chapter, on the outside of the outline write some descriptions that represent what God wants for you. Now, inside the figure, write a prayer, song, poem, or story about those things becoming a part your life and who you are as one of God's own.

nine

I've always been able to trust people,
but it was the opening up part I had problems with.

The weight of the rocks in the bag tied to Colin's ankle pulled him toward the bottom of the lake. He fought and thrashed but watched the blue sky and the surface of the water swirl farther and farther away. He could still see the shadows of his enemies on the shore laughing—enemies he had battled for years. They'd won.

Colin, who had fallen asleep on his bed, jerked awake and sat up. *No. They can't win.*

The guilt over his choice to turn to the Internet and to porn again and again tormented him. He'd tried his friend's suggestions, had attempted to be accountable. He was doing better, not visiting those sites online as much. Filters and accountability helped when he used them. But sometimes the pull became too strong, and it was easy to get around those. He gave in. Then even when he stayed away from it, it was hard. He was tired of having images of the women he'd viewed flash through his mind when he least expected it—like when he was talking to friends or sometimes even at church when he was trying to worship.

I can't handle this alone. I don't know what else to try.

Though youth group that night was upbeat, for Colin it seemed to drag. Lately it had a different feel to it too. The size of the group had grown too large for the old room. They were trying out a new program in the church's main worship center.

During worship, Colin mechanically ran his fingers across the keyboard. He felt drained, hopeless. Thoughts of the continued battle over his choices crowded into his mind. He had been doing everything he could to beat his addiction to porn. He fought. He lost. Weariness and discouragement hung on him like worn, heavy armor.

When worship ended Colin left the stage, soul weary and spent. He dropped into his chair, willing himself to get through the service so he could go home. He didn't want to fight anymore. He listened to his youth pastor's message. It didn't relate directly to his struggles, but the Bible verses Mike shared soothed his spirit and called to him. He didn't have to stay in that deep, lonely place. God had provided people who could help. He just needed to let them know.

> He fought. He lost.
> Weariness and discouragement hung
> on him like worn, heavy armor.

I'll talk to Mike.

After the meeting, students gathered around the youth pastor, talking, asking questions, joking around. As Colin helped break down the stage backdrops and the equipment, he watched for an opportunity.

Man, how am I going to do this? Colin viewed his youth pastor as someone who had been a close mentor to his oldest brother, but Colin had never had that kind of connection with Mike—

or anyone for that matter. Still, he looked up to him, considered the huge impact he'd had, not only on his brother and other students, but on his own life too. He guessed Mike probably had no idea. Now, when he was finally ready to share some of who he was, he was revealing the darkest parts.

Colin gathered up the cords for the keyboard and microphones. When he turned around again, Mike was there at the stage, picking up his notes from the talk he'd given that night.

His eyes met Colin's. "Hey, good job tonight."

"Thanks." Colin's heart began to beat hard. This wasn't easy, but this was his chance. "Um . . . can I talk to you about something?"

"Absolutely." Mike smiled and waited.

"No, I mean . . . not right here."

"Yeah, sure man. Let's go . . . " Mike scanned the room. Some of the other teens were pushing back the dividers that made the room smaller during the meeting. Colin followed his gaze until his pastor finally pointed toward the other side of the church sanctuary. " . . . to the back there. Out of the way."

"OK."

The two of them walked to the seats that angled upward, giving a bleacher feel to the back rows. They sat down in the front row of one of the sections.

"So what's up?" Mike looked casual, but concern and compassion were all over his face.

Colin tapped his fingers on his leg. *Where to start?*

"You know in your message, you talked about . . . " Colin started out wide, talking about the night's message, hoping to gain courage as he circled in toward what he really wanted to say.

They talked for a while, and finally Colin took a deep breath. *Time to go for it.* "So that made me think about the way I've been living."

It was true. A lot of what his youth pastor taught really did make him think about how he lived and how he spent his time. And he was beginning to no longer feel that porn was just something lots of people do; he was definitely seeing it as something more than just a pastime he couldn't control. It was out of control. Definitely out of *his* control.

> **They talked for a while, and finally Colin took a deep breath. *Time to go for it.* "So that made me think about the way I've been living."**
>
> http://

"So, um . . . what I wanted to talk to you about is . . ." He fidgeted with his hands and stared at the back of the red-cloth chairs across the aisle. His pastor was quiet and didn't push. "I've had a problem with looking at . . . um . . . pornography." There—the truth was out. Someone he saw face-to-face knew the truth.

Mike ran his hand through his hair. "Wow, yeah. That's a tough one."

"Yeah." Colin looked up toward the ceiling but not at his pastor.

"How long have you been battling this?"

"I've been doing it since before junior high—all online. I just wanted you to know I was struggling with it, cuz, like, I really want to stop and I need some prayer."

Mike put his hand on Colin's shoulder. "Yeah, you've got it. Let's do that right now."

> **He sat there, taking in the fact that he'd just confessed something really difficult. He began to feel hope that this could be defeated.**

Over the next few moments, Mike prayed fervently for God to heal Colin's mind and heart, and to break the hold pornography had over him. He prayed for strength and a willingness on Colin's part to fight the battle.

Colin prayed too, and they both closed the prayer with an "amen." He sat there, taking in the fact that he'd just confessed something really difficult. He began to feel hope that this could be defeated. The enemy hadn't won. He sensed a lightness of soul he hadn't felt for a long time.

Several weeks passed. Mike checked with him and at times gave him some ideas of ways to think about other things at moments when it was hard—like turning to prayer or purposely diverting his eyes and focusing hard on something completely different.

Colin liked the accountability. He talked to a few others he felt close to, confessing his addiction. Others knowing about his struggle made him feel it was more possible to overcome it. They knew, and he'd feel that if he ever slipped up again.

nine

His online friend Mike knew about it, since Colin's being open started with the survey that went to Mike, and Colin had told Steve. One day, he told Kelly in a chat:

Kelly: I'm proud of you for being done with that habit
Kelly: :-)
Colin: yeah, me too
Colin: well . . . hopefully done, i cant say that im fully done
Colin: guess what else? even though i have failed with what was in the past, i think God was giving me a second chance. wednesday night im going to lead worship at my youth group
Kelly: *grins*
Kelly: awesome
Colin: you dont realize how awesome it is

Colin thought about that. It felt good to know he was a part of something, contributing to what was going on at his youth group. He felt closer to God, felt like he wasn't alone in his battles. This could work.

But he was about to discover that he was hanging on by the thread of things going well in his life. It was a thin rope and the slightest fray would send him spiraling down once again into the depths of sadness and the traps of online comfort.

> Encourage one another daily, as long as it is called Today,
> so that none of you may be hardened by sin's deceitfulness.
>
> HEBREWS 3:13

FACE-TO-FACE ACCOUNTABILITY

It felt like a huge relief. Colin no longer had to carry around a secret. Others knew, and it was OK they knew. Still, he had needed someone who was not only aware of his struggles but could offer support and challenge. Turning to his youth pastor wasn't easy. Here was someone who had known Colin for a good chunk of his life. Though he trusted Mike, it still took courage.

Mike remembered it being a big deal for Colin to take that step of trust. But then, what to do with it? He said, "Believe it or not, this had not come up a lot with kids yet. We talked about it in youth staff, that it was something brewing, kind of a subterranean-type thing, and that we were going to see a wave of kids sooner or later who had this issue. We knew that a lot of our boys, if maybe not most, were having some kind of exposure to it, but it was still a time of 'What do we do with this? How do we help these kids?'"

Mike wanted to be there for Colin but felt he didn't take it as seriously as he could have at the time. He realized later, "It wasn't a struggle in my own personal life, and that's a great thing. On the other hand, without personal experience, you tend to not understand how big a deal it can be for people. I think a lot of us don't have any grasp of what takes place in the brain chemically that creates that addiction. It really becomes this monster that, like any other true addiction, causes it to turn into a true physiological craving in the brain."

From Colin's perspective, his youth pastor was there for him in a huge way. He remembers Mike asking him how he was doing, and the main thing, besides the face-to-face friendship, was "he was someone else who knew."

> Educate yourself about the dangers of pornography, including the physiological dependency that's created from viewing it. As available as it is, you can bet that you know young men *and* women who are struggling. Talk to your pastors about ways to address the issue in your community or church.

CONNECTIONS

Online and alone. Being at the computer allows us unlimited opportunities to network and connect with people all over the world. But the price for this, often, is that we have physically isolated ourselves. We might stay that way for hours.

Even if we have some social contact, for every hour we're sitting in front of the screen, that's one less hour we could have been connecting more deeply with someone at home or in the community. And one more hour that we might be heavily engaged in one of our personal Internet traps with little or no accountability.

We need people in our lives. We need face-to-face connections. We were created by God with faces and voices and physical bodies for a reason.

Johan put it this way: "Internet activity is bad when it diminishes our ability to engage with real human beings, and instead we engage with their digital shadows."

Many say they still have a social life. Tyler said he hung out with friends and had a great social life, but he also easily spent seven hours at a time online—on his favorite networking site, playing WoW, or at times viewing porn. When Tyler was deep into that, he would have denied he had a problem. He believes most would. He said, "They're going to say, 'I do have a life, and I do have a social life,' but they're basically just lying to themselves."

He's now found a deeper satisfaction in his real-life friends. "There's a different feel when you're talking to someone in person. When you're with people, spending real time with them, you're getting to know them on a deeper level."

Though Kelly, one of Colin's friends, values her online friends, she said, "I think exclusively having online friends isn't a great idea because you miss out on a lot." She likes when some of her online friendships have moved toward letter writing and phone calls and visiting each other during summer breaks. *Big* caution here—these situations are only safe and healthy when they are carefully chosen and monitored, and parents and trusted adults are kept in the loop. Kelly makes sure she does that.

Katy enjoys online chatting, but she said, "There is a certain depth that my friends have that my virtual buddies lack. My real friends know me very well and can listen to me and relate to how I'm feeling."

Ryan, who often presented himself far differently online than who he really was, said, "You get drawn away from life, unable to interact with people. That becomes your reality and the outside life becomes absent." He suggests "building relationships based in reality and letting people see you for who you really are instead of the facade you make online."

Johan talked about his moments of going on the Internet to view porn—even if only for a brief few seconds: "When I've been online, I come away with a sharpened sense of what I was *not* made for. I was not made for digital interaction and cyber-satisfaction."

No matter what we're doing online, when the time or activities become excessive or step into dimensions God never intended for us, we are missing out on those deep face-to-face connections we're all created to share. Real-life and God-honoring relationships.

> Take a good look at the groups you lead or the relationships you have and consider how you might be encouraging online communication more often than face-to-face. Do you rely on e-mail to communicate with students? Use a networking site to spread the word about events? Instead, plan ways to communicate the same information and messages in person and to go after more in-person connections.

Search mode. It's not just a small box we fill in and click to find information. It might also be our frame of mind as we go online for escape, adventure, or connections. We're searching, and the Internet seems to offer a quick and easy way to find what we want or feel we need.

We can become so drawn in by the virtual satisfaction of our needs and desires that we miss the adventure of seeing how God might meet those more deeply in real life. When we spend hours immersed online, we are left with little time to:

+ enjoy the world around us;
+ stir up our God-given passions for life and what's beyond online;
+ use the body and mind he gave us in moving, interacting, and connecting with people face-to-face;
+ take the time to contemplate what we can see and experience away from our computer monitor, discovering the thrill of the use of all five of our senses.

God created the world and then he said "Look!" (Genesis 1:29, *NLT*). It's as if he were saying, "See all of this. I made it for you to not only take care of but to use and enjoy." Romans 1:20 says, "Since the creation of the world God's invisible qualities—his eternal power and divine nature—have been clearly seen, being understood from what has been made." By experiencing God's creation, we see him and know him at greater depths. Not through online images, but firsthand with our eyes and our senses.

God also had in mind our face-to-face connections with people. We are created with bodies to work together, play together, and worship and serve God together. Romans 12 even includes a metaphor of the body to show how we can each contribute to the community of people who serve God:

"In this way we are like the various parts of a human body. Each part gets its meaning from the body as a whole, not the other way around. The body we're talking about is Christ's body of chosen people. Each of us finds our meaning and function as a part of his body. But as a chopped-off finger or cut-off toe we wouldn't amount to much, would we? So since we find ourselves fashioned into all these excellently formed and marvelously functioning parts in Christ's body, let's just go ahead and be what we were made to be" (Romans 12:4-6, *The Message*).

"Chopped-off finger" or "cut-off toe"—pretty graphic interpretation of this verse. What it means is, *you* are important and missed when you're not participating in relationships and God's community as you were designed to do. Get your whole body and mind back into life. Join in. Connect.

> *God, I'm really missing out on a lot when I sit alone at my computer, especially when I'm expecting that my needs for connection or excitement can be met digitally or virtually. You made an amazing, intricate world and planned for people to see each other, to hug, and to laugh or cry together. Nothing on the computer can compete with what you've created for us to enjoy. Resharpen my senses and my desire to experience it all.* AMEN.

> **What a wildly wonderful world, God!**
> **You made it all, with Wisdom at your side,**
> **made earth overflow with your wonderful creations.**
>
> Psalm 104:24 (*The Message*)

GOING DEEPER

▪ Have you had a difficult experience that has hurt you and that now keeps you from making good connections with people away from the computer? What are some ways you can begin to change that pattern?

▪ Be intentional about joining in with life away from the computer. What is one way you can do that this week?

■ Think of a good, safe friend (of your same sex) whom you often talk with online and who is living in the same city you are. What can you do together to begin to build a stronger in-person friendship?

DEEPER STILL

God *did* make a wildly wonderful world. Grab your camera or video camera (if you don't have one, borrow one) and step outside. Go to some favorite places and new places. Talk to people. Ask questions. Take pictures of God's creation. Journal about what you've discovered.

ten

This was my major test of faith. Moses had his desert moment. David had his desert moment. Jesus had his desert moment. God tested all three there. This was my desert moment. I felt very alone.

THIS CAN'T BE HAPPENING.

Colin shut his bedroom door and slouched into his desk chair. He and Nique had been talking for days, and finally the decision was made—they were breaking up. Over the two years they had been dating, they had gotten close—maybe too close. He knew some parts of their relationship weren't healthy for either of them. Now her mom was pushing for the breakup. He agreed to it.

He jerked his jacket off. *Didn't mean I wanted it.*

> He and Nique had been talking for days, and finally the decision was made— they were breaking up.

Colin felt the old pull of loneliness. He clicked open a browser window, opened up a flash game site. He wanted to get lost in something and forget how he was feeling. After a while, he started a chat with a couple of friends, told them about the breakup. They sympathized and tried to encourage him. He still felt the growing heaviness.

Going into automatic mode, he started clicking around online. He visited a couple of blogs and message boards. It killed more time. None of it helped. The familiar desire to look up porn returned for an instant but flickered away when he remembered encouragements from his online friend Mike and from his youth pastor. He steered away from it this time, though the old draw was still a constant battle.

Nique. She won't be here for me anymore. Their friendship would change. They'd been together for more than two years. Now they wouldn't be talking every day like they used to. He missed her already.

And it's my senior year. We made plans for things to do when we graduated.

Colin's stomach knotted.

How am I going to do this?

Several months passed. Colin's loneliness and depression pressed in. Getting through each day became a chore. He was trying, but he felt the gaping hole the breakup had left.

He turned up the volume on his computer speakers. Recently he'd picked up some new CDs. While he clicked aimlessly online, he listened to the lyrics of a popular punk rock band. They pounded out lyrics of the pain felt when someone you care about is far way. *Far away. Nique couldn't be farther away.* He missed her and an ache squeezed his chest. He couldn't think of anything else.

Colin chatted and posted on the message boards as the CD faded into a song about someone being the reason for making changes, a reason to show who you really are. *Nique, I miss you. I made so many changes for you.*

He sighed and slumped into his chair. He was getting back into spending hours online . . .

Glancing at the clock at the lower corner of his monitor, Colin realized it was time to go to youth group. He didn't want to go. Didn't want to see Nique. Didn't want to talk to anyone. And lately he hadn't, though he still went every week. He'd go tonight too. He slipped out of his chair, grabbed his jacket, and headed out into the chilly November night.

They pounded out lyrics of the pain felt when someone you care about is far way. *Far away.*

http://

At that night's youth service, Colin played with the worship band, then sat down in a chair off to the edge of the room. After a few months of trying out youth services in the main worship center, fewer were showing up. The meetings were back in the old fellowship hall. They had a different feel of late; this one bordered on tense. Pastor Mike had set the lights low. The selected songs were more mellow than the usual upbeat and sometimes rowdy songs.

Then Mike stood and walked to the stage. He seemed quiet, preoccupied. He pulled a stool over and sat down. No icebreakers or games tonight. His expression looked serious. Something was up.

"A year and a half ago, I began to feel a change inside. I didn't know what to think. Burned out? Distracted? I even examined myself to see if I was dealing with some sin in my life."

Colin watched his pastor's face. He seemed to be laboring to tell this story.

"I prayed, fasted, read Scripture, and sought counsel." His pastor's shoulders rose and fell in a sigh as he continued to share the month-to-month struggles he'd been through during the last year. Finally he said, "God is calling me out." He stopped for a moment, seeming to take in reactions and finding it difficult to go on.

Colin sat forward. *What is he saying?*

> **Colin felt his body tense.**
> **His face warmed. He was confused,**
> **then angry, and then panic set in.**

Mike went on. He felt strongly he wasn't to continue as their youth pastor. Someone new was coming. For a while he and his wife would continue to serve in the church. He wasn't sure what was next, but still felt that his life was set apart for ministry.

Colin felt his body tense. His face warmed. He was confused, then angry, and then panic set in. *You belong here. You can't leave. You're the one who's supposed to make everything better in my life.*

His body shook with denial. He tried to focus on what was being said. *I don't understand. No one is asking you to leave. Why are you?* He almost wanted to beat against his pastor's chest, to plead with him to reconsider.

Mike went on, trying to prepare them for the changes that were coming. "We'll do everything we can to make a good transition. God is in control. You will learn things you never could have otherwise."

> **God where are you in this?**
> **Are you abandoning me too?**
> **Silence. He couldn't feel God at all.**

Nothing feels in control. I keep losing the people I care about or have opened up to the most, the only ones who really know me.

Mike encouraged them to grow in their faith. He talked about a trapeze artist and the need to let go of one bar to grab the next. But for Colin, all this talk wasn't helping. He felt like he had just missed grabbing the swing and was now falling with no net underneath to catch him.

Growth, progress, blessing was promised, but he couldn't see it. He felt abandoned. *God where are you in this? Are you abandoning me too?* Silence. He couldn't feel God at all. He believed he was there—refused to doubt it—but God seemed far away. He sighed. *It's my fault, God. That's where I've kept you all along—at a distance.*

The worship band was called up to play a closing song. Colin followed the others to the stage, but he felt numb. He didn't look at his pastor. He played the keyboard, hardly noticing the song or the words. The depression that had already taken hold in the last months began to make its full claim on him. An image of God reaching out to him flashed through his mind—and then was gone. He was spiraling to a dark place inside where he'd keep everyone—God included—at a distance.

ten

> Do not be afraid or discouraged, for the Lord will
> personally go ahead of you. He will be with you;
> he will neither fail you nor abandon you.
>
> DEUTERONOMY 31:8 (*NLT*)

CAUGHT OFF GUARD

Unknown passages. Unexpected traps and enemies. Loss of valuable resources. In a game, you can never be sure what's going to happen and what's around the next corner. Even more true in real life.

Colin wouldn't have guessed that two people he had come to rely on for their support and friendship wouldn't be there for him anymore. It shook his world. "When Nique and I broke up, I was *very* depressed. We had been dating for more than two years."

That relationship ended and then was followed by his youth pastor's announcement that he was leaving. Colin pulled away from people at school and at church. He said, "I still sat with people. Just didn't talk for a while." Everything was changing. What felt comfortable was gone.

"Mike was someone I had just started developing a relationship with. He had taught me so much about God and my relationship with him. I knew I could talk to Mike. Now suddenly he was leaving. I was crushed." The changes took their toll. "I sunk back into the depression. I regressed and had a hard time adjusting."

He reacted, in part, by gravitating back toward the Internet. Chatting, playing games, mostly killing time, escaping—all of it only contributed to the loneliness. He found himself easily caught in the cycle he'd been in before, with the depression and his Internet use each feeding the other. This time, though, he was sacrificing newly established friendships and connection to life. "The more I was involved with the Internet, the more depressed I became, the harder it was for me to keep relationships and friendships alive."

He counted on those friendships to keep him going in a good direction, but he'd soon learn that only one friendship—with God—was unshakable and could set him on a solid forward course.

Mike remembered many details about those months when he and his wife wrestled with the decision of whether he would continue as youth pastor. Nothing had happened. No one was asking them to leave. They had just felt it was time and that God was moving them on. He said, "We'd seen so many people leave, and it was just like a grenade went off, and we were saying, 'Dear Lord, help us to do this right.' And yet still, it was like, this is just hard."

He recalled the mixed reactions from the night he told the youth group. "Colin was definitely in that group of kids that I think probably looked at us either with tears or a blank stare, going, 'What do you mean you're leaving?' It was hard."

Tammy, one of the youth staff, thought back to a meeting at the church when Mike and his wife were talking about making the announcement: "We were in Mike's office. He really felt leaving was the best thing, and he gave all the reasons. And he said, 'The hardest thing about this is leaving Colin because he is doing so well.' No one said Colin was fragile, but there was a real concern. Mike had really connected with him."

Looking back, Colin said, "I had grown up with this man, and he shaped a lot of who I am. I had no idea that this was all in God's timing."

He would soon begin to see that God had not abandoned him. He really was the friend who would *always* be there for Colin.

> Watch for those who seem to easily get taken under by life events and emotions. They could be more likely to withdraw and turn back to online obsessions to cope. Take them out for something to eat or for a coffee. Give them an opportunity to talk.

STAYING ON TOP

Battles. Real life ones can be tough. And if you're fighting against any kind of Internet obsession, taking healthy steps away from it requires planning and support—along with the commitment to win the battle.

Here are a few strategies from those who have been there:

Set a timer or ask someone to help you get off the computer after a certain amount of time.

Commit to making "bye" your last comment—and mean it.

Challenge yourself not to be on the computer more than you absolutely have to—start with an hour limit. As you're successful, increase your challenge. Share your goals with a friend.

Distance yourself from the computer by reading, watching a movie, doing artwork, cleaning or organizing, schoolwork, anything to keep your mind off the computer.

Do something physically active, like weight lifting or running.

Take a walk around the neighborhood; join a sport of some kind.

Read, go bowling, go to a movie, hang out with someone.

Schedule your time. Get a job. Keep yourself busy.

Use software that shows exactly where you've been, or use strong filters or blockers. Have an accountability partner who is committed to checking in with you.

Make it a regular practice to honestly confess sin to friends and mentors. Be just as open about temptation when it hits.

Avoid going online when you're home alone.

Don't have your computer in your bedroom.

Memorize Scripture.

Choose ideas that fit your particular situation and battle. Talk them over with a friend and commit to them. If nothing on this list would come close to helping, then it really is time to get others involved.

Tom Neven, editorial director for Focus on the Family's Youth Outreach, had this advice: "As with any addiction, admitting you have a problem is the first step. Getting others to help you is next. Don't be afraid to ask parents, siblings, friends, or your youth pastor to hold you accountable. Don't keep it a secret!"

Get God involved too. He's definitely aware of what you're battling.

> Talk with the teens and young adults you know about activities away from the computer that can help beat the tougher obsessions. Have someone type up a list of all these great suggestions and hand a copy out to everyone. Do this several times a year and keep the dialogue going.

FACING THE BATTLE WITH GOD

Our online battles may be intense or subtle and deceiving. Either way, they are destructive. Not only do they impact us mentally, emotionally, and at times physically, but also spiritually. Our faith and relationship with God become essential in the fight.

Ryan isn't sure about his faith in God and where that fits into his life, particularly in the healing of his deep hurts and his battles with the Internet.

"Right now, I'm searching and asking questions, just trying to find him," he said. "Faith is a hard thing to grasp. I've gone through my entire life relying on myself through problems. The thought that there's something out there I can give my problems to and have them lifted off more easily, to say, 'God, I can't do this, take it away. I can do all things through you'— it doesn't seem possible right now. I want to, but I just don't know how yet."

That's being honest.

Maybe those like Ryan, who are wrestling with their faith, can pick up some encouragement from Mike, Katy, and Johan.

They've discovered that God is with them in the battle, and they have a part in moving forward to win it.

Mike:

I say, "God, help me to get rid of the sin that is against what you've created for good. When I go online and do some of the things I do, I'm taking what you've created for good—your design for our minds and bodies—and making it evil. And that obviously is not pleasing in your sight, and I want to be pleasing to you in any way that I can. Please help me to get rid of the sin that is so easily entangling me."

Some verses that share more on these thoughts: 1 Corinthians 6:18; 2 Timothy 2:12; Psalm 34:14; Romans 8:8; Romans 16:19; Hebrews 13:20, 21; Hebrews 12:1-6

Katy:

Be in the Word constantly. That's the main weapon we Christians have. It's good to know plenty of Scripture for every temptation we face. It also encourages you to not give up hope and know that you can still move on. Another thing too—prayer. Wow, what a mighty weapon! Things can start changing in our lives if we only humble ourselves and pray. You can find your strength in the midst of your greatest weaknesses.

For more: Psalm 119:15, 16; Ephesians 6:10-18; 1 Corinthians 10:13; 2 Chronicles 7:14; 2 Corinthians 12:9, 10

Johan:

I have found that my actions are the outworking of what I've decided in my mind. So when a thought or a temptation presents itself to my mind, I stop right there and confess, "God, I cannot overcome this in my own strength. Please put my sinful nature to death and empower me to obey you." Taking these thoughts captive and making them obedient to Christ is pivotal.

For more: Proverbs 22:5; James 5:16; 1 John 1:9; Isaiah 12:2; Romans 6:6, 7; 2 Corinthians 10:5

Joshua, in the Bible, is a hero who wouldn't go to battle without God. This Hebrew leader was preparing to take his army into what seemed to be an impossible and deadly encounter (Joshua 1). They had to fight and they had to win. If they didn't, they would never take possession of the land and life God intended for them. God told Joshua and the Israelites that he would not leave or abandon them (v. 5). He encouraged them to "be strong and courageous" (v. 6), and to obey his Word and not "turn from it to the right or to the left" so that they would be successful wherever they went (v. 7). God offers those same combat words to us today.

You have a battle to fight. It's real. It's intense. Get God involved and keep him involved. Determine to stay on track and move forward. Be strong and courageous.

God, sometimes I forget you are here with me and ready to take me through my battles with strength and courage. Teach me and remind me—so that I remain committed to moving toward the victory and freedom you have planned for me. Through the Scriptures, make the truth of who you are clear to me. Deepen my faith so my convictions become immovable when the battles come. AMEN.

> Put on the full armor of God, so that when the
> day of evil comes, you may be able to stand your ground,
> and after you have done everything, to stand.
>
> EPHESIANS 6:13

GOING DEEPER

■ What life events, emotions, or thoughts make you more vulnerable to returning to destructive or less effective ways of coping?

■ What can you plan to do now that will help prepare you to handle those differently next time?

■ God can handle your doubts and the questions about him, but it's important to face them. Write down three doubts or questions you have about God, and then, as soon as possible, talk about them (in person!) with someone you respect.

DEEPER STILL

Katy, Mike, and Johan's battle plans came right out of verses they knew from the Bible. Look up some of the references listed underneath what they shared. As you read through the verses, create your own statement of faith and commitment about your personal battles—online and off.

eleven

I was ready to call it quits on my faith completely. Not because I doubted my faith—I knew God existed and no one could change my mind about that. But it's very hard to live halfhearted.

"THIS IS AARON. HE'LL BE YOUR YOUTH PASTOR. Let's give him a welcome." Mike led the applause as the new guy took his place on the stage.

Colin glanced around. Some looked excited and joined in the clapping. Several looked like they wanted to bore ice holes into the new guy with their frozen stares. Colin didn't feel anything. Just numb. Resigned to the situation. He slid down into his chair and crossed his arms.

"Hey, thanks. I'm looking forward to getting to know all of you."

> **Memories nudged his thoughts, memories of an existence full of choices made *for* him. Can't I *ever choose how anything goes?***

Colin watched Mike sit down. *This is it. He's not our youth pastor anymore.* He felt his eyes burn and his chest tighten, especially as the new guy began to talk about how this was a big change for all of them.

"It's in the middle of changing seasons that God brings people to a new destiny," Aaron said.

I liked the old destiny better. I was cool with it. It was comfortable. This felt so out of Colin's control. Memories nudged his thoughts, memories of an existence full of choices made *for* him. *Can't I ever choose how anything goes?*

The message continued as the new youth pastor talked about the stories of Moses and Joshua. "In each case, a new leader was brought on to take the people to another level. I'm praying that's what God will do through me here. I take that responsibility seriously. Together we'll see where God takes us."

All Colin knew was that *he* wasn't going anywhere—with this pastor or anyone. And, as he was only beginning to believe, he wasn't sure he was going anywhere with God.

The next Wednesday night, Mike didn't come. Colin felt hollow as he played the keyboard through the worship service. He didn't care anymore.

He sat down, made it through the announcements, ignored the icebreaker game, and prepared to endure the new pastor's message.

> **Aaron told how he had been into a bad lifestyle, trapped in addictions, and never went to church before he was twenty-two.**

As Aaron stood, Colin began to notice the physical differences. This guy was tall but slightly shorter than Mike. His hair was lighter, and he had a stockier build.

"I want to give you some of the background of how I came to Christ." Aaron told how he had been into a bad lifestyle, trapped in addictions, and never went to church before he was twenty-two. He related his life in some ways to the prodigal son that Jesus talked about. "When I came to God, I was just a broken nobody, a young adult running the streets."

Colin shifted in his chair. *Wow, way different from my experience—going to church my whole life, living in a comfortable home.*

"Like the prodigal son, I had nothing to offer God. Just 'Here I am. This is all I've got.'" The pastor's voice grew warm, passionate. "We don't need to bring anything to God. All we need to do is show up. And God, the loving Father, will take us, put a robe on us, and restore us from our brokenness. He'll point us to a new destiny."

Colin pulled his arms tighter across his chest. *That destiny thing again. I don't have one. And if I did, it's not here, and it's not with God.*

A song began to play, one that told the story of the prodigal son. Colin watched as the pastor took on the role, reenacting the story on the stage, stepping down into the aisles. The pastor's face showed the full range of emotions, going from the carefree, happy son spending his inheritance to the despairing man, far from his father and his home.

Colin felt somehow he could relate. *I've lived in my home. I haven't left it, but I know that hopelessness.*

The drama continued. Aaron pantomimed with the music. The prodigal returned home, hoping his father would accept him as a servant. He had nowhere else to go. When he came down the road nearing his home, his relieved father ran to the road to meet him and welcomed him back into his home as his son. Tears streamed down Aaron's cheeks.

There's something about this guy and his faith. Maybe if he could do it, not even growing up in the church . . .

The song ended. Aaron called the worship band up to play and offered a time for anyone to come up front for prayer.

Colin took his place at the keyboard. Questions ran through his mind. He felt confused and tired as he slumped down on his stool. He pushed through his weariness to finish the song.

> **There's something about this guy and his faith. Maybe if he could do it, not even growing up in the church . . .**

As he stepped away from the stage, the words from the drama still hammered through his mind: "The only time God ran was when he ran to me."

I don't know, God. Can I believe you care that much about me?

A few days later, Colin stood at the door of the youth room, talking to Aaron. "I'm tired of being lukewarm about my faith. I can't live halfway anymore. Isn't it better to be cold than semi-on-fire?"

"What do think? What do you believe about God?"

Colin looked at the new youth pastor. Aaron's eyes look pained as he waited for an answer. Colin glanced away and focused on the door jamb. "I believe in God. I believe Jesus is the Son of God and that he's God in flesh. I believe it all." He shook his head. "I just don't think I can give my whole self to God."

Aaron didn't ask why. He just waited.

Colin brought his head back up and focused on the lights in the room, squinting through his glasses and letting the light refract and break into rotating beams. He really didn't have anything else to say. He was thinking about quitting church entirely but wasn't sure he wanted to tell Aaron that.

Yeah. This was it. No one would ever change his mind about God's existence. That part couldn't be shaken. But he was turning eighteen in a few months. It was time he made his own decisions. If he was just going to keep living like he was, keeping God at a distance, he might as well give it up— even if it meant losing out on everything God might have for him. The relationship had to be all or nothing. He was leaning toward nothing.

> I greet you with the great words, grace and peace! We know the meaning of those words because Jesus Christ rescued us from this evil world we're in by offering himself as a sacrifice for our sins. God's plan is that we all experience that rescue.
>
> GALATIANS 1:3, 4 (*THE MESSAGE*)

A LOOK INSIDE

Colin had run down a winding and difficult passageway and hit what looked like a dead end. There waiting for him was a mirror that reflected the inside of his heart. He couldn't ignore it anymore, and he couldn't pretend.

He said at that time that he "meant to completely stop going to church." He was almost eighteen and about to graduate from high school. "It was time I started making decisions for myself instead of letting my parents decide my faith for me." At seven, he had made a genuine choice to follow Christ, and then while dating Nique, again made that commitment. But he says that second time was "just as much to impress her as it was to actually get close to God."

Changes were good, but he realized it wasn't enough. He'd cleaned up his language. And through accountability with his online friend Mike and his youth pastor Mike, he was gaining some ground in his battle with pornography. But he said, "Those were like rules I was trying to stop breaking. Rules fix nothing. I needed Jesus most of all."

Around the time that Mike left his youth pastor position at the church, Colin had decided to give up his faith. The last thing he planned on was getting to know the new youth pastor. Colin was leaving, and that'd be it. But then he listened to Aaron's story of where he'd come from and how he'd come to know God. "I didn't relate to most of it, but it was the passion in which he said it. Something about him drew me to him." Colin thought that if everything the man said was true, he *had* come a long way. He was clearly different. A part of Colin wanted to say, "If he could do it, I could definitely do it. I definitely can change." Still, he wasn't sure.

One thing more certain, though, was that he had a growing sense that Aaron might be someone he could connect with. Looking back, he knows it was one way God reached him. "I'm convinced that if I had been the only student hurting in the youth group, and I was the only reason Aaron was brought here, God still would've done it."

> God could be using you in someone's life in ways you'd never guess. Look for such a person, such a possibility. Be ready to tell your story, to reach out, to be available.

HANDLING THE SETBACKS

Colin had made a lot of great progress and done some of the right things in tackling his porn addiction. Then, as he connected more with the youth group, his time online began to naturally move toward a better balance. In many ways he no longer saw his Internet use as an addiction. But anytime he slid into a depression, he bumped up his online time, where he could escape and talk to friends. It had become a way to cope, and he withdrew from life yet again.

Setbacks happen. Once we've resolved that we're making changes, when a wave hits and knocks us down, it's easy to turn back to the old stuff. And if it hasn't been all that long, even something as simple as boredom can draw us back.

Elize, who struggled with online gambling and spending, experienced this. She said, "When I get bored, I am right back at it. I sometimes think that the boredom will always win over my knowing not to do it. I hope that I will never get to a point where I turn to stealing money to be able to gamble online." She does feel strongly that, with God's help, she won't get to that point: "I know there is much more to life than that. I know I will beat this online addiction with the help of God." She's right. And since boredom is different for each of us, God can help us identify ways to creatively use our time, including ways to serve him by helping others.

Sometimes our setbacks are a struggle of will and the desire to keep our commitments. We might get tired of the fight and let things slip. Tiffany explained what most easily sets her back: "The struggle is to keep Internet use to a reasonable level and not let it come before more important things. Sometimes I'm not very good at resisting the temptation to talk to people online too much."

The guys who have battled porn addiction commented on the reality of the continued struggle and setbacks.

Nate realized there was more to it than just deciding he was going to stay away from porn sites. "I'm never halfhearted. I soon learned that the Internet was too much for me." He realized that though a determination to change was important, doing it on his own wasn't enough. "I didn't pray and I should have. I thought I could reduce my time and do it on my own, but I was playing a mind game with myself."

Tyler strongly recommends using a filter to prevent setbacks. "I guess there are people who have the self-control to do it without a filter, but for me, I need a filter because I *will* look it up. You know, if I'm alone in the house, and I'm not doing anything, I get that urge to sin. Staying busy for me is a good thing."

Johan realized he'd turn back to pornography again and again if it were left to his own willpower. "It soon became apparent that I was not able to defeat my flesh through self-discipline and self-control." He felt that a filter is only part of the bigger picture for him: "Release from Internet addiction is not about installing a safe search engine or restricting viewable sites or any of these tools. At its heart, addiction is about the flesh that is bent on destruction, and victory is about crucifying the flesh."

We can honestly face what we're dealing with—our weakness and the addictive nature of what we're drawn toward—and then be determined to work toward change, with full awareness that with God we can win each battle.

When we slip and lose one, we can remember God is there and ready to set us back on our feet. Johan said, "I don't beat myself up when I fall. Instead, I return to him and allow him to restore me, and together we keep on walking."

> **Live wholeheartedly. Be the example that someone else needs. When struggles or setbacks hit, don't fake that everything is OK, but show how you walk through it with determination and faith in God.**

JESUS—THE ONE WHO RESCUES

We see pictures of the gentle Jesus talking to children or holding a lamb across his shoulders. But he is also a warrior who fights for you. He is the one to run to, to trust your life to—online and off. Who is Jesus? He is:

Mighty God (Isaiah 9:6)

Prince of Peace (Isaiah 9:6)

Redeemer (Isaiah 41:14; 54:5)

eleven

Lord of Our Righteousness (Jeremiah 23:6)

Immanuel—God with us (Matthew 1:23)

Friend of sinners (Matthew 11:19)

Good teacher (Matthew 19:16)

The true light (John 1:9)

Lamb of God (John 1:29)

Messiah (John 1:41; 4:25)

Gift of God (John 4:10)

Good shepherd (John 10:11)

The way, the truth, and the life (John 14:6)

Deliverer (Romans 11:26)

The power of God and the wisdom of God
(1 Corinthians 1:24)

Life-giving spirit (1 Corinthians 15:45)

Our hope (1 Timothy 1:1)

Mediator (1 Timothy 2:5)

Author and perfecter of our faith (Hebrews 12:2)

Lion of the tribe of Judah (Revelation 5:5)

In a relationship with him, he is all of those to you and more: "Once you were like sheep who wandered away. But now you have turned to your Shepherd, the Guardian of your souls" (1 Peter 2:25, *NLT*).

We can have game heroes, Internet idols, and chat friends we bare our souls to, but the only one who can *guard* our souls is Jesus. Your shepherd and guardian. Your warrior, hope, and deliverer. Wholeheartedly bring him into every area of your life.

God, I often don't see it coming, and I trip up again. Thank you that when I do, you don't turn your eyes from me. When I'm tired of my mistakes and falls and doubting the changes you've begun in me, you are there to remind me that you will continue the work you've begun. The battles will be won. AMEN.

I am certain that God, who began the good work within you, will continue his work until it is finally finished on the day when Christ Jesus returns.

PHILIPPIANS 1:6 (*NLT*)

GOING DEEPER

■ When you've worked at changes in your online choices, have you also experienced setbacks during that time? Try to identify what happened that led to getting off track. A difficult relationship? A disappointment? Something as simple as just allowing yourself to get bored?

■ Boredom can easily be avoided by planning ahead and making a list. Ask God to help you find ways to serve and to give. For example, clean out your closet and donate your stuff to charity, or find out how you can help at a local soup kitchen or homeless shelter. What can you put on your list?

■ Each time we slip up, we have a choice to give in to our habits and weaknesses or to get back on track with our commitment and our relationship with God. Instead of just waiting to face that moment of decision, what can you plan to do so that you experience more consistent success?

DEEPER STILL

Using the different names of Jesus, the Bible verses, and some personal thoughts, create cards to place near your computer. Look at them often as you think about how Jesus is present with you all the time, desiring to help you with your toughest battles. If you'd like, look up his other names. There are plenty more.

twelve

I was hesitant about going at all, then it really made a difference.
I began to be myself a lot more. I began to be more whole.

"WE'RE DOWN TO THE WIRE. If you're going to sign up for the winter retreat this year, we need your forms today."

The retreat was coming up fast. Colin watched as youth night continued and a few of the teens performed a funny skit about how great the retreat would be. He was dead set on not going. Not with everything that had happened with Nique. She'd be there and it would be hard. Colin crossed his arms. *Why should I go?*

As Aaron highlighted some of the details and talked about how it would be an amazing experience, Colin thought about the last three retreats he'd gone to. They had their high points. Definitely were up there in intensity as some of the best emotional and spiritual experiences he had every year. But when he came home, everything went right back to being like it was before.

I'm not going.

Since the breakup, he had pulled away from his friends. And he'd pulled further away from God. He still wasn't sure where he wanted God to fit into his life, if at all.

When the dates were announced, he realized his birthday would land in the middle of the retreat. He imagined what it would be like to stay home. This would be the first birthday in a while he didn't spend with Nique. He wrestled with all of this.

Stay at home and do nothing, or go to the retreat and be miserable because she's there? Great choice. He let out a long breath. *I'll think about it.*

> Since the breakup, he had pulled away from his friends. And he'd pulled further away from God. He still wasn't sure where he wanted God to fit into his life, if at all.

A few weeks later, Colin was back at the Gold Rush Lodge, dropping his duffle bag by his bunk. He looked around at the familiar rustic setting. The large dorm-style rooms had plain white walls, with lines of bunks with blue mattress covers.

A couple of days after the youth service, he'd gone to talk to Aaron and told him he was willing to give God another shot. He also agreed to go to the retreat. Nique wasn't coming, so that made it an easier decision. His fourth year at the retreat. He had some hopes, but the doubts and the lingering depression outweighed those.

It's just going to be another one of those experiences that I leave behind in these mountains.

The theme for the weekend was telling your friends about Christ and seeing that as a lifesaving privilege. Colin thought about the few times he'd actually tried to do that with his friends. Except online, where he could say anything he wanted, he didn't talk much about Jesus with friends who didn't know about God. At school, that included nearly all those he hung out with. They'd started figuring out he was a Christian, but God didn't come up much in their conversations.

That night, Colin sat in a chair at the back of the room in the lodge, watching a video clip from *The Return of the King*. Frodo was hanging on the edge of a cliff ready to fall to his death in a pit of fire in Mount Doom. His good friend Sam was reaching to grab his hand. "No. Don't you let go!" Frodo struggled to hold on to the edge. Sam encouraged again. "Don't you let go. Reach!" Their hands met and Sam pulled him to safety.

> ### It's just going to be another one of those experiences that I leave behind in these mountains.

Colin knew where this was going and guessed how it fit into the weekend's theme. Earlier in that night's meeting, Pastor Aaron set up a lifeguard-training scenario and urged the students to care about telling their friends about Jesus and salvation. He'd pretended to be a lifeguard saving a mannequin and, with plenty of laughter from the group, gave lots of comparisons to their part in saving a friend. "A good lifeguard wouldn't sit there and watch someone drown," he'd told them.

Then he talked about Isaiah, a prophet in the Bible. "He had a kind of lifeguard challenge presented to him by God. In Isaiah 6:8, God asked him, 'Who will go?' Isaiah had a choice. He responded, 'I will.'"

Next he'd played the clip of Sam helping his friend escape a death in the fiery abyss.

twelve

As Colin took all this in, he thought about his friends—especially those who didn't know God. He did care about them. *But can I have that kind of commitment to God?* He still wasn't sure.

The next night, Aaron and the youth leaders had created a dark and smoky effect. They set up eerie lighting to turn the stage into something representing Hell.

Colin sat off from the others toward the back and settled in to watch what they were going to do with all this. A CD began to play over the speakers, a monologue of someone who had woken up in Hell. He was writing a letter to his Christian friend, wanting to know why he wasn't told about his need for God and his forgiveness. One of the youth acted out the torment, while others rattled chains in the background. The story began, "Josh and Zach were best friends."

Colin was impressed with the stage effects. The youth leaders did a great job.

> **Colin found himself searching for answers, for direction from God, for the connection he'd longed to have, most of all to grasp God's purpose for him.**

As it went on, he felt drawn into the drama, thinking about his friends, thinking about his own life. Aaron wasn't trying to scare them but challenge them to care enough to reach out a saving hand. Colin wondered, *Do I?* As the story came to the end, he realized that his heart was pounding hard. He wiped his eyes. *When did I start crying?* He didn't know.

The room grew quiet. Very quiet. Aaron stood in front of the scene. "This wasn't real, but Hell is." He reminded them about the question given by God to Isaiah, "Who will go?" Then he told them about Jesus calling the fishermen to be his disciples, calling them to leave their nets and become fishers of men. "So my question to you is, who of you will go? Who will commit to doing what it takes to be that lifeguard, that Sam, that Isaiah? Who will say, 'Yes, I will be that friend. I will go'?"

He pulled out fishhook necklaces made of cord. Over the next few moments he called all of them to pray and consider their commitment and, when they were ready, to come forward.

Many were on their knees praying, some crying. Colin found himself doing the same, searching for answers, for direction from God, for the connection he'd longed to have, most of all to grasp God's purpose for him. It had to be more than just getting through each day. So far that hadn't worked all that great.

Colin got up from the floor and found himself walking toward the front. *God, I don't want this to be an experience that I feel now and don't commit to later. Help this to be real for me.* He stood in front of Aaron who, eyes filling with tears, smiled and nodded at him. Colin bent his head to receive the necklace. As Aaron placed a hand on his shoulder and prayed for him, he felt God asking him the question. It was time for an answer.

Who will go, God? I will.

Colin crunched across a grassy knoll and stopped to look out over a pond. This one, somewhat secluded, was a ten-minute walk from his house, through the neighborhood and down some back roads. He never saw anyone there enjoying it, but he liked going there—especially lately.

As he often now did, he listened to a mix he created for his iPod that he labeled "Pond Worship." The fading daylight triggered a nearby streetlight to switch on. It cast its glow across the water. The winter air chilled Colin through his hooded sweatshirt, and he pushed his hands deeper into his pockets.

The worship music playing through his earphones seemed to invite him to join in praising God. He began to sing out loud. Then he grew silent. So much had happened over the last few months. Some big losses and disappointments. Discouragement like he'd never known. He'd even almost abandoned his relationship with God entirely.

> As the setting sun radiated fiery colors across the sky, he grew quiet. He felt it as deeply as anything he ever had—he wanted never again to be a Christian just halfway.

This time, coming off the winter retreat, he felt different. *God, you were there all the time. You're with me now.* He began to pray that his faith would grow, that the call to care about the souls of others around him and in the world would never fade. He prayed for his community, for his nation. He felt the urgency for his generation to be diligent, to be true lights that represented Christ's message of salvation. He glanced up at those lights now illuminating the pond. *Brighter than any streetlight, God.* Then he prayed for specific people in his youth group and family. Though he had kept them at a distance so much of his life, he felt how important each one was to God. And to him.

EYES ONLINE : EYES ON LIFE

As the setting sun radiated fiery colors across the sky, he grew quiet. He felt it as deeply as anything he ever had—he wanted never again to be a Christian just halfway.

> **We know that in all things God works for the good of those who love him, who have been called according to his purpose.**
>
> ROMANS 8:28

A NEW QUEST

Warm and real, God's presence soaked into Colin's life and poured out in expressions of hope and vision for his future.

A retreat experience prompted the change. He saw that decisions at previous retreats had been real to him at the time, but then didn't stick. It could happen again. "You're in a room with a bunch of other Christians who are hurt and broken like you, and all these emotions flood over you at once. You'd be willing to make any decision for God."

But he wanted his decisions this time to mean more. "What I did when I got home was different. I was determined not to let another camp experience just fade away. I started taking my Bible out. Started reading, started memorizing Scripture. Praying. Worshiping." And that genuine connection with God began to make a real change inside Colin. He caught hold of the message Aaron gave, a message he felt God was giving to many of them, but *also* included him. He began to feel a passion to reach teens like him. Now, several years later, he looks inside and sees that what happened during that weekend took root. Colin says, "It's still there."

> Don't assume someone who walks through the church doors every week, who participates in activities or worship, has taken what he knows about God and made it personal and life-changing. Pursue depth with your friend. Ask. Make your conversations real and impacting.

THE STRENGTH OF PURPOSE

Colin longed to know that his relationship with God was personal and genuine—more than a habit he had because he'd been in church his whole life, more than a response to an expectation. When he grabbed hold of the realness of that relationship, he was also beginning to discover purpose. There was reason and intention beyond his own world as he had known it. He had something to offer. God had something for him to do.

When we get a sense of our purpose—God's purpose for us—we are more likely to put time and energy toward that goal. It naturally will set off a change in our decisions, including our online choices.

Ryan, who was abandoned by many of the important people in his life, turned to the Internet. It was there. When asked what he thought about God's purposes for him, he was again extremely honest about God and his online choices. He said, "Right now, I'm still searching. It seems like it would be easier if I had God because I'm not strong enough to make changes on my own. I don't have a strong enough will. To just be able to give it to God and say, 'I need you'—that would be that extra strength I need to do it. It would help me know morally what is right and wrong. With God you feel like he's watching you and he's right there with you and makes you aware of what's going on."

You could be one of those who meets Ryan in a chat room. You could even be someone who's "there" for him and talks to him about God, encouraging him that, yes, God could be his strength. But what Ryan needs is someone like you *in* his life, face-to-face, who will be that one person who won't abandon him. He needs to hear your voice, see the concern in your eyes, feel your presence, and know you care. Without that, Ryan won't learn to trust anyone. Maybe, least of all, God.

There are lots of Ryans out there who are hurting and searching, who need someone like you to be a face-to-face friend who shows him love, who *shows* him Jesus.

That's a purpose to grab hold of.

> **Heartfelt passion for God and the needs of the world is contagious. When the teens and young adults you know watch you, do they see that in you? If so, help them begin to catch that vision by involving them in active ways.**

MADE FOR PURPOSE

We are created to have meaning. Each day we search for it and hope for it—most of the time hardly aware that's what we're doing. We feel good when something happens that hints that we might have some importance to our existence. And if we're not sensing that, we'll do something to create it and make it

twelve

happen. As limitless as the Internet seems, it has limits in giving us purpose.

We find that ultimately through our relationship with Christ. Colossians 1:16 says, "Everything, absolutely everything, above and below, visible and invisible, rank after rank after rank of angels—everything got started in him and finds its purpose in him" (*The Message*). It only makes sense. He created us. And we are created for a purpose greater than anything we can imagine. It's a purpose we can trust.

Part of that "purpose in him" involves loving others. Jesus, just before he went to the cross, said, "So now I am giving you a new commandment: Love each other. Just as I have loved you, you should love each other. Your love for one another will prove to the world that you are my disciples" (John 13:34, 35, *NLT*).

That kind of love is an action—an intentional, face-to-face, in-person expression of the deep love of God. It definitely extends beyond the confines of four walls.

There's a whole world out there. Who will go?

God, today can be hard enough that I'm not sure I want to think too far beyond it or the next day. But you have so much more for me to think about and do, so much for me to be beyond the limits I've placed on myself. Take me deeper into a real and personal relationship with you so I can know you better, so I can hear you more clearly. Show me where you want me to go. I will go. AMEN.

> The Lord will fulfill his purpose for me;
> your love, O Lord, endures forever—
> do not abandon the works of your hands.
>
> PSALM 138:8

GOING DEEPER

■ Have you had experiences of getting close to God that seemed to fade later? What would make a difference for you in getting the realness of the relationship more deeply rooted in your life?

■ When we really grab hold of our purpose—God's purpose for us—we are more likely to put time and energy toward that. Have you begun to sense some strong interests that could develop into ways you can serve God? What are those interests?

twelve

■ List as many ways as you can think of to use those interests in your home, church, and community.

DEEPER STILL

Ask God to show you a specific project you can do to care about those in your community—to put "love into action." Meet with a Christian mentor, youth leader, or pastor who can help you think through some of your ideas and give you prayer support. Get another friend involved.

thirteen

*When all was said and done, and I graduated from high school,
I looked like a completely different person. I was happy—
happy to be out of high school, happy to be a part of something
bigger than me, happy to be in God's grace and living in his will.*

COLIN SLID ONTO A BENCH on the front lawn of his high school.

Aaron pulled a small, worn, leather Bible out of his back pocket before he sat down. Colin's youth pastor then laid it on the bench between them, along with some papers and a pair of scissors. Then he leaned back and rested his arm across the back of the bench.

Colin looked at the scissors and wondered what his youth pastor had planned.

Aaron smiled. "So how's it going?"

"Goin' OK."

The retreat had been a turning point for Colin. He felt he'd finally figured out his commitment to God. He was going for it. Since that time, Aaron had approached him and several other teens and asked if they wanted to be a part of the youth leadership training. The plan was that they would meet once a week during lunchtime. Colin was the only one at his high school, so it had turned into one-on-one time. OK with him. He loved hanging out with his pastor and was growing to respect him as his mentor. Sometimes they got together during other times too.

"Yep, things have been going pretty well," Colin added.

"Great." His pastor was quiet for a moment. "How 'bout the Internet stuff—how's that going?"

Colin had checked in with Aaron regularly about his struggle with pornography. Sometimes he had to admit that he'd slipped up, but he always told his pastor the truth. No reason to lie. This time he could say he was doing better.

> His pastor was quiet for a moment.
> "How 'bout the Internet stuff—
> how's that going?"

"I still think about it once in a while, but I feel like with God I'm overcoming it more and more. You know how it is."

"Yeah, I really do." Aaron shook his head. "Can't do it without God—no way."

His pastor had shared similar struggles with him and was able to relate how it made all the difference when he became a Christian. He had become a great accountability partner for Colin. For a moment they were both silent, just sitting back, enjoying the breezy spring day.

"So what are the scissors for?"

"Oh, those." His pastor picked them up along with a piece of paper. "I've got a challenge for you—sort of a game."

Colin sat forward. "OK, I'm into challenges like this. I'll try it."

"I want you to figure out how you can cut a hole big enough in this piece of paper so you can fit your whole body through it without ripping the paper."

"OK." Colin took the piece of paper. He turned it different ways. Folded it, unfolded it. Almost made a cut, then stopped. He looked at his pastor. "I know it's gotta be possible. Just don't know how yet."

Colin made some cuts. Thought he was onto something. Then he realized he'd started all wrong and what he'd tried wasn't going anywhere. He held up the cut paper to show his pastor. "That didn't work."

Aaron laughed. "Good try."

"I know it's possible though."

"Exactly. And I'm impressed. You're the only one so far who has tried. From the start, you didn't doubt or say it was impossible."

Colin grinned.

Aaron took a fresh piece of paper, folded it in half lengthwise, made alternating partial cuts across the paper, then snipped the inside fold lines. He held the paper up, and it fell open into a giant circle.

Colin laughed. "*That's* how you do it."

> **Colin thought about that. He'd seen what it was like to do things on his own and fail, pretty much like trying to squeeze through something as small as the eye of a needle.**

"So this can be applied to our faith." Over the next few moments he flipped the pages of his Bible to different Scriptures and stories about doing the impossible.

Aaron stopped and pointed to a page. "Here in Matthew 19, Jesus tells his followers it's easier for a camel to go through the eye of a needle than for someone who is rich or feels like they have it all together to enter the kingdom of God." He looked at Colin. "Jesus told them that, yeah, it's impossible for man, but it's not with God."

Colin thought about that. He'd seen what it was like to do things on his own and fail, pretty much like trying to squeeze through something as small as the eye of a needle. He couldn't beat down the addictions—not only to pornography, but also his obsessions with anything to do with gaming or being on the computer all the time. He'd turned to all of it trying to escape loneliness, sadness, or a lack of purpose in his life. God had helped him see something far better. And he'd begun to discover that the freedom and purpose that seemed impossible, even a few months before, were now possible.

A year and a half later, Colin sat in a chair next to his youth pastor's desk. While Aaron finished a phone call, Colin glanced around the room. It was filled with all kinds of stuff to look at. He remembered sitting in the same office with Mike when he was working there. He missed Mike, missed looking at the hundreds of pictures on his bulletin board. But he was also glad Aaron was here. He'd become not only a mentor, but a good friend.

Aaron nodded to Colin, gesturing that he was almost done with the call. Colin nodded back.

He leaned his elbow on the arm of the chair and propped his head. Across from where he sat was a laminated one-year calendar that took up nearly the entire wall. His youth pastor had scribbled ministry and family commitments in many of the boxes.

The offices seemed to be a place for each of the pastors to express their personalities. Aaron, obviously a huge Scooby-Doo fan, had jerseys, ties, a lunchbox, and even a big stuffed Scooby in the room—somewhere. Colin stretched his neck to look toward where he'd seen it last, then guessed it must be stuffed in the corner.

He'd been in the office often through the last year, especially after graduating from high school, when he'd started volunteering. He worked ten hours a week helping with anything that needed to get done for the youth meetings.

It was now summer, a year later. The air conditioning was cool, but it felt good since he'd sprinted the several blocks from his house. He wasn't sure what the meeting was about. He only knew that when Aaron had called earlier that week, he was pumped about something. All he'd said was not to make any huge decisions about the next year, that he had something he wanted to talk to the senior pastor about and then get back to him.

His pastor hung up the phone. "Hey, Colin. Sorry about that."

"No problem." Colin sat up and turned toward his pastor.

"So you're probably wondering why I was so fired up."

"Yeah."

"Well, you know that my associate youth pastor is leaving and that opens up a spot. I talked to the senior pastor, and he agrees. Instead of trying to find a new person, we want to take you on as an intern. You'd be doing a lot of what you've been doing as a volunteer with student ministries, but you'd work more hours and we'd pay you. What do you think?"

> **"Instead of trying to find a new person, we want to take you on as an intern. You'd be doing a lot of what you've been doing as a volunteer with student ministries."**

What did he think? Beyond the volunteer time at the church, he'd just been putting in hours at a local retail store's photo department and not liking it at all. Aaron knew that.

"That's awesome!" Colin felt energized and was ready to say he'd start the next day. Even right that moment.

Aaron brought him back to earth. "Keep it quiet for now while we work out the details. We'll get you started in a couple of weeks if you want to do this. If you do, go ahead and give notice at your job."

Keeping it low key would be hard, but Colin was grateful for the opportunity. "OK, thanks. Wow."

It was the big kick-off event for the new school year. A giant blow-up obstacle course filled one edge of the church parking lot. Though junior high and high school youth group had met together for a few years, this year Aaron had split them into two groups. Tonight Colin was helping with Xplosion, the junior high group. The whole place swarmed with students.

Some of the adult leaders stood in pairs or groups, watching and chatting and manning the barbecues or passing out food. Colin walked around among the junior highers talking and joking with them. A few of the guys greeted him with friendly punches in the arm. He smiled and said hi or mockingly punched them back or chased them down after they'd thrown a punch and sprinted away.

He turned when he overheard one of the boys challenge another to a race through the obstacle course. Colin watched as they dove through a hole and then pushed their way through a cluster of air-filled columns. More obstacles followed before they climbed a net and came down the other side on a slide.

> **Colin felt energized and was ready to say he'd start the next day. Even right that moment.**

The challenger won and stood there laughing.

Colin stepped up. "Hey, think you can beat me?"

"No problem."

"Alright, you and me—let's do it."

The two of them dove through the hole into the course. Colin bumped and scrambled through, getting to the other side, beating his young friend by a few seconds.

"Hey man, take that." Colin, out of breath, grinned.

Another one watching said, "I'll take you on."

Colin laughed. "OK. Bring it on."

> Create in me a pure heart, O God,
> and renew a steadfast spirit within me.
>
> PSALM 51:10

LEVELING UP

When Colin walked the aisle at his high school graduation, he realized that the person he had become was far different than the person who had stepped on campus four years earlier. He had more to learn and conquer, but he was willing. The changes he'd made, especially in the last half of his senior year, were sinking deep. Colin would never be the same.

Looking at that time, he said, "God got ahold of me. I became a completely different person. I talked to people. I made new friendships. On top of that, my relationship with God started to flourish. I was able to worship freely. I prayed more. I read my Bible. I was starting to become someone people could look up to, and I really and truly believe that it was all God."

With the help of God and those he placed in Colin's life, the pull of pornography was lessening. Today, Colin is realistic that it's an addiction, and he knows he has to be careful. He says, "It's not controlling me anymore. I can usually stop if I see myself going down that road. I know God is in the process, and I have faith that there will be a time when pornography will no longer be an issue at all."

His online use also changed. He said, "I don't remember really going on the Internet as much after this time." He still used the Internet. He was a tech assistant at school and fixed computers, and he still had interests and online friends, but these were no longer consuming all of his time. He said, "Youth group became really important to me. I talked more often to people I didn't know at youth group or in class. And instead of being this socially awkward kid, I could actually connect with people."

And that continued. During the year following graduation, anytime he wasn't working he was volunteering and helping Aaron with the youth group. Aaron said, "He had no expectation of getting paid, never asked. He just came because he wanted to be around ministry and he wanted to serve." It was an easy decision for Aaron to ask him to join the staff as an intern. Aaron said, "He had definitely earned it—just showing his heart and willingness to volunteer."

More changes came. The Colin who hated interacting now reached out to the students, played with them, raced them, did all kinds of things to interact. He says relating to students, seeing how they're doing, and joking around now comes naturally. He laughs and says, "Shuffle Your Buns is now one of my favorite games." One of his favorite tricks is to change up the game by switching seats with someone across the circle instead of next to him.

But Colin is also modest. He said, "I wouldn't call myself a leader or role model. Looking back, I can see God preparing me for the leadership I'm involved in today, and if it weren't for what little I did back in high school, I doubt I'd be so involved with youth now."

One thing is for certain: he sees that God never gave up on him. "Anytime I felt hopeless, or felt like God wasn't there, he was listening and not abandoning me. Putting things in perspective, God was there the whole time."

> Look for potential in the students and young adults you know and don't hesitate to tell them what you see. A few simple words can make a huge difference and turn a life in a new direction.

PLUGGED IN

Colin was still online some, but the difference was that now he was fully connecting with life. God was a huge part of that picture—drawing out, healing, and transforming the hurt that sent him to the Internet and freeing him from the obsessions that had trapped him there. It was also his relationship with God that naturally impacted balancing his online choices. He was now looking beyond the Internet for purpose and fulfillment.

Kelly believes strongly that involving God in your choices should be the same whether online or off. "Just like your relationship with God should be reflected in the places you shop, the activities you do, the music, movies, and books you immerse yourself in, your relationship with God should affect where you go online."

Erin feels it's crucial to keep her relationship with God a priority and does that by making sure she spends time with him daily. "I know when I don't, my day is all bad," she said.

Tyler has struggled with making sure God is in his thoughts throughout the day. He said that when he plays WoW, he doesn't think about God, and he emphasized, "I mean, *at all*." And he doesn't see that as a good thing. "There's a problem right away. God should always be on your mind. You get heavily into what you're doing. It does confuse you, and it causes that separation."

Nate has tried this: "I imagine Jesus sitting right next to me, looking at my screen. I can't hide it. He knows what I'm looking at, and he knows my heart."

And there's the offline side of the picture—getting immersed in life, like Colin did.

Katy said she's doing pretty well now. "So far, so good. I'm getting involved in others' lives and being a part of the bigger picture. I'm on my way back to a healthy online life and more of a real-life future." For her, that included developing deeper friendships and getting involved more at school.

Tyler said, "I'm involved with a church, and I have friends who go too. I do a lot of group activities."

Johan believes healthy relationships are key—especially with his wife now that he's married. He realizes that "Marriage is what sexuality was meant for. It was meant to open up to us some of the deepest connecting available to a human being."

Marius hangs out regularly with friends and family. He also said he "spends more time with God, reading and studying the Bible as opposed to spending those hours playing games that did not glorify God in any way."

Connecting with life. Balancing online choices. God-directed purpose and fulfillment. A very cool way to live.

> Help a teen you know use her computer skills and interests in creative ways in ministry. Explore ideas with her and make other connections with people who can help her use her talents.

An Amazing Intervention

In the darkest and most difficult moments in the clutches of a trap, we may wish we could be zapped right out of it, never to struggle again. It doesn't usually work that way.

Though God can do that, in his wisdom he most often begins the work deep inside of us, often before we see changes in our outward choices and behavior. It happens at that moment when we recognize the reality of our spiritual need and, by faith, come into relationship with him. That work that he begins inside, however, *is* miraculous.

2 Corinthians 5:17 says, "This means that anyone who belongs to Christ has become a new person. The old life is gone; a new life has begun!" (*NLT*).

New. Completely different. Better than the old—because the old is gone. An amazing transformation of the heart. It's a mystery that is difficult to comprehend but that we can be sure God accomplishes within us.

We are wrapped in flesh and its tendencies toward our own desires, so more often we see our failings. We catch only small glimpses of the transformation God has begun.

But that will grow. You'll notice it more and more. Keep your eyes on God and on the life he has for you. What he has begun inside will soon begin to flow into every part of your life. You'll see.

> *God, I want all that you have for me in life. Give me a greater desire and vision for the fullness and freedom I can experience by being connected to you and to the world you've placed me in. Show me my heart and my need. Give me the faith to trust you to create a new heart within me. I want the adventure of watching that newness spread into every part of who I am and what I do.* AMEN.

I'll give you a new heart, put a new spirit in you. I'll remove the stone heart from your body and replace it with a heart that's God-willed, not self-willed.

EZEKIEL 36:26 (*THE MESSAGE*)

GOING DEEPER

■ In thinking about further balancing what you do online, consider a way you can go deeper than you ever have before in connecting to God. For instance, increasing daily time studying his Word or worshiping him or meeting to pray with someone weekly. What will you do differently this week?

■ Immersing ourselves in life also means connecting with others. Name a friend you see often who you can begin to encourage on a regular basis.

■ List one or two things you've seen God changing in you since you began reading this book. These could be big things or small things—something as big as beating an addiction or as seemingly insignificant as changing how you view one part of your day. Don't discount how God works, even in subtle ways.

DEEPER STILL

Sometimes we need to take a break from being busy and wrapped up in things to really see the condition of our hearts before God. It's important to include regular spiritual checkups, no matter how long we've known him. Go somewhere different than the places you usually go—a state park, a hiking trail, the track at a school, a quiet pathway. Ask God to show you where you are, how far you've come, and where you're heading.

EYES ONLINE : EYES ON LIFE

fourteen

Why didn't anyone do anything to reach out to this young man?

COLIN SAT IN THE SOUND BOOTH in the back, operating the computer while a friend worked sound. As he did more often lately, he had programmed slides to help transition from one part of the youth service to another.

For tonight's youth group he'd timed a few funny comments to pop up at different times behind what was happening on stage, and that got everyone rolling with laughter. He smiled. He enjoyed making the students laugh. Then it was time for the offering message. Tonight he was giving it.

He went to the front. Taking the mic and holding it in front of him with both hands, Colin looked out over the group of fifty teens. He knew what he wanted to say. He wasn't nervous.

> **Colin reached the corner of the room and turned. "This is where he sat . . . every week."**

"I want to tell you about a guy I knew about five years ago. He was very shy, wasn't very well liked." Colin began walking slowly across the room as he talked. "People would try to get him involved at youth group. He didn't want to be there."

Colin reached the corner of the room and turned. "This is where he sat . . . every week."

He described how uncomfortable the student felt at youth group, sometimes so much that he'd be in tears. As Colin talked, he walked back toward the center of the stage.

"He kept coming even though he didn't want to be there. Week after week. Year after year. There was a point in his life when others saw potential in him and reached out. He started to become someone people kind of liked."

The room was quiet. Every eye was on Colin. He was sure they had no idea who he was talking about.

"He gave his life to God and started getting involved in youth group. Did really well. He graduated from high school." Colin shook his head. "But he didn't leave."

Colin continued the story, telling how the guy started helping out at the church and became a youth leader.

"He wanted to use his life for God to serve other people. I happen to know all this"—he paused a moment and looked at different ones around the room—"because this person I'm talking about is me."

Colin heard different reactions, whispers, even gasps.

> **"You may not have liked me or wanted to talk to me. I wouldn't have blamed you. I didn't like myself."**

"This is a completely true story. I honestly was one of most hurting kids you would have ever met. You may not have liked me or wanted to talk to me. I wouldn't have blamed you. I didn't like myself. But because I let God take over my life and now live for him"—Colin pointed to himself—"you see this person today."

No one made a sound.

"I want to end with this verse from 2 Corinthians 5:17: 'If anyone is in Christ, he is a new creation; the old has gone, the new has come!' Let's pray."

> **He guessed there was at least one person—maybe many—who could relate to the old Colin.**

Everyone bowed their heads while Colin prayed, thanking God for being there with them, for dying on the cross, and for making it possible for lives to be transformed. "Thank you for getting rid of the old stuff and making us new. Amen."

He stepped off the stage. Some continued to watch him as he passed. He guessed there was at least one person—maybe many—who could relate to the old Colin.

Several months later, Colin sat at his desk just outside Aaron's office. With his earphones in, he listened to his Switchfoot mix. His hands were flying over his computer keyboard as he worked to finish up his video.

"Hey, Colin. You didn't hear what we just said, did you?" Giggles came from nearby cubicles.

Colin pulled off one earphone. The women working in the office at the church were at it again—talking about girl stuff and forgetting that a guy was in the room.

He laughed. "Nope. Had my earphones in."

"Good." They laughed and lowered their voices.

He put the one earphone in again, leaned back in his chair, and let the video run. One by one, photos of individuals came up and stayed up for a few seconds before transitioning to the next—the victims of the Virginia Tech campus shooting. He shook his head. *So many victims.* Thirty-two killed. A spring morning. A campus transformed by evil.

He pushed his glasses up on his nose and pulled his quirky ball out of the drawer again. The ball blinked as he tossed it between his hands. When the video played out, he set the ball down and leaned forward. With ease, he rearranged some of the photos and clips and synchronized the edits with the song he'd chosen, "How to Save a Life" by The Fray. This was to be a tribute to the victims of the Virginia Tech shooting.

Just a few more tweaks. He added one more picture at the end—the shooter's. *His life was lost too. Did anyone reach out to him? Maybe things could have turned out differently.*

> **He realized how crucial it was
> that people chose to reach out to him.**
> *Man, that made all the difference for me.*

He thought about his own life. Though he was sure he never would have gone down a violent road, he realized how crucial it was that people chose to reach out to him. *Man, that made all the difference for me.*

A hand came down on his shoulder. It was Aaron. Colin pulled off his earphones and dropped them with his iPod onto his desk.

"Let's see what you've got."

Colin replayed the tribute. They'd planned to show it at youth group that night.

"Yeah, looking good. Thanks for doing that."

"No problem."

"Come on in my office and let's go over what we're doing tonight." Aaron turned and headed toward his office, already talking. "So, what I'd like to do . . ."

Colin pushed away from his desk and smiled. Things felt right. It was good to be a part of something. Good to be making a difference.

> **We are God's masterpiece. He has created us anew in Christ Jesus, so we can do the good things he planned for us long ago.**
> Ephesians 2:10 (*NLT*)

BRIGHTER THAN ANY STREETLIGHT

Colin was reaching out to the people around him, connecting, caring about others. With God's truth growing inside him, he was becoming the light he had prayed to be—brighter than any streetlight.

He said, "I never really noticed until now how many of my prayers God answered."

Now Colin is a youth leader at his church for both the junior high and high school groups; he's active in media projects and music. He said, "I have the opportunity to speak into young people's lives on a regular basis."

fourteen

Colin's next-door neighbors, the Jennings, noticed the changes. Patty Jennings, the mother, said, "There's huge maturity over the last three years. He's finding relationships, getting involved, knowing who he is in Christ no matter what he does, what he's thinking, or how he's feeling at the moment."

Tammy, on the youth staff, has known Colin since he was a small boy. She said, "He's made huge, huge progress. He's definitely secure. Has been really motivated in ministry. He relates to the kids and is sensitive to the hurting ones."

Colin is continuing his internship at the church and taking Bible classes and college classes as he can. More recently, he and others at his church were trained to work within some local high schools to address the issues of depression and suicide. He goes with his team to high school assemblies and then, in follow-up, confidently goes alone to individual classes to talk with students.

Doug, Colin's dad, says, "His ability to draw from his experience and willingness to share is telling in the sense that he's gotten past a lot of things. He's done such an excellent job of communicating. It's really amazing. He's got a commitment to working with youth, but the fact that he's gone into a situation where it's more than a bunch of church kids . . . it's a big, big deal."

Colin puts students at ease as he shares about his experience with depression. He also engages them in discussions to come up with solutions to respond to a friend who is depressed or suicidal. Students who might be struggling know he understands. Others learn the importance of encouraging their friend to get help. He said, "I really needed it. Looking at the warning signs that I talk about now, looking at what I went through, I was definitely crying out for help. Thankfully, I got it."

Also, given the right situation, he doesn't mind talking about his struggles, and about how tied into his depression the Internet had become.

Along with his work with teens, he has the opportunity to use his computer interest and skills in his work and ministry: "Because I was so wrapped up in the Internet and then delivered from it, God has been able to use me while still doing the things I love." Colin realizes how much happier he is now. "I'm online, but it's not all I do. I've found that balance."

You can too.

> As someone who is influencing the lives around you, it's important to have a sense of making the most of your time and becoming all you were meant to be in Christ. As you grow in these areas, those who are watching you will grow too. Bring them along with you.

MORE EYES ON LIFE

Others who told their stories for this book shared what they hope for as they continue to work toward engaging more fully in life:

Ryan said his hope is "to have a stronger connection with friends and family and just to be able to reach out to youth and my younger siblings and help them so they don't go through what I've gone through. I want to give them what I've learned in a way they can relate to."

Tyler: "I just want better things now, where before I didn't care. I had settled for what I had. Now I know that God has plans for me. I know I can achieve more because Christ does that in me. I have potential to shoot higher." Tyler wants to aim for giving 100 percent to whatever he does: "Do it with everything you have. Not just your job. It could be anything—doing dishes for your mom, writing a paper for your teacher, doing chores, or investing in a relationship."

Marius wants to start a ministry. "My goal is to preach the gospel to the city of Johannesburg and reach out to the homeless and poor in the city."

One of Tiffany's biggest gifts is music. "I'd like to be able to play more for people," she said.

Katy is gifted in handling horses, so she sees that as part of her future. She also said, "I have a heart for young women like myself." She feels God is leading her to teach and minister to young women and to address the issues they face. She said, "That won't happen for many years, but I'm beginning to live out God's plan for me." She also enjoys using dance in her community as a way to open doors to start conversations with girls.

Johan wants to get a dialogue going in his community about the problem of pornography. He said, "I figure that if we are able to speak to one another honestly and without judgment, then more and more people will find a way to freedom." He has definite goals for his life that not only affect his present, but also his future and into eternity. He shared, "I want my Father to cast an eye back over the life I have lived in his sight, and I want it to bring a great big grin to his face. Essentially, when I'm living purely, all of my time and energy is to be invested in these two loves—love for him and love for his people. Even my time on the Internet needs to center around these things."

A passionate, invested life—that's what each of these individuals desire.

Jeremiah, an Old Testament prophet, lived that kind of life. God told him, "Before I shaped you in the womb, I knew all about you. Before you saw the light of day, I had holy plans for you" (Jeremiah 1:5, *The Message*). God had set him aside for his eternal purposes. And Jeremiah wasn't an old man when God let him in on the plan. He was a teen.

With God's help, Jeremiah, later known as "the weeping prophet," quickly grasped what was at stake—the lives of thousands. From that day on he refused to waste one day of his life. He couldn't. The passion within him ran deep. God continued to give him a heart to see the destructive paths in many of the lives around him and a voice to cry out a strong warning. Knowing that God promised to be with him through every step (Jeremiah 1:8), Jeremiah did that wholeheartedly, regardless of the cost to him.

Before each of us is born, God knows about us too. Before our first breath, he may even have a specific holy plan for our lives, something powerfully meaningful and important for his purposes that we can be passionate about.

Once we're able to step away from what consumes us or traps us—no matter what it is—we begin to gain a greater sense of what our lives can count for. Having our eyes on life means embracing everything God has for us. Life is happening right now.

Make it count—now and for eternity.

God, in creating me you have given me the gift of life. Instill in me a deeper sense of how I am to live it out and make it count. AMEN.

May the God of hope fill you with all joy and peace as you trust in him, so that you may overflow with hope by the power of the Holy Spirit.

ROMANS 15:13

GOING DEEPER

■ What do you hope your life will look like in being part of the community around you? How can you be immersed with friends and neighbors in a Christlike way?

■ Think about your interests, gifts, and abilities as not only present but also future characteristics of who you are. To be sure they are a *strong* part of your future, what is one practical step you can take this week to make sure you are putting time into developing them?

■ If you had the power to do something different with the Internet and change how it impacts people, what would you choose? Consider one small way you can make a difference in this way this week. Now dream big—how might you become part of something really huge and life-changing for many?

DEEPER STILL

Write about what you want your future to look like—make it as long or short as you'd like. What steps can you take to work toward that vision? Tell someone who can encourage you along the way. Consider some way to physically represent that commitment. Write a poem and share it with someone else. Maybe it's planting a tree to symbolize your goals. Or speak to a group and challenge those listening to join you with their own commitments.

fourteen

A LETTER FROM COLIN

THE PROBLEM WITH INTERNET obsession is that you can look completely normal and nobody knows you are in so much pain. That was true for me. When I was consumed by the Internet in junior high and high school, I was so depressed, and nobody ever knew why. They didn't even begin to think it had anything to do with the computer. As I grew older and was able to look back on my life, I could see that the Internet was a big reason why I was depressed. It just continued to feed my miserable feelings, never letting me breathe for a moment.

If you've been there, where you feel like you can't handle it anymore, then picking up this book was a great first step. But don't just leave it at that. You need people in your life to keep you going, people who will ask the hard questions at the hardest times, people you can trust.

God promised that he will finish what he started in my life, and he promised the same for you too, so don't ever give up.

Don't try to do this alone. God doesn't expect you to.

A LETTER FROM JAN

THERE ARE MANY GREAT THINGS about the Internet, but in these pages I chose to write about the traps and about individuals who've walked into those snares. If you've read this far in the book, you know their stories. You may not know that the most important part of this book for me has always been *you* . . .

. . . because you matter greatly—to those who love you and especially to God. You are worth fighting for and not allowing anything to get in the way of all you can be and are becoming. *Anything*—including those Internet choices and activities that slowly rob you of the amazing identity, relationships, or connections to real life God has in mind for you.

You also were the reason why this was a tough book for me to write. I knew that for some of you it might be extremely difficult or frustrating to think about what you're doing on the Internet. I see the huge battle in that, and while I wrote, that was constantly on my mind . . . and in my prayers.

It is my hope that some thought, Scripture, or story within this book stirred you to begin to want more for yourself, to begin to move out of any of your personal online traps—whether just beginning or huge battles—toward the best that God has for you.

It is a courageous journey. I pray that you take it.

Jan

RESOURCES

The Web

WWW.CHOOSE2LIVEFREE.COM

This Christian site for teens and young adults provides up-to-date Web resources and links that go along with the issues discussed in the Live Free books. Recent topics include self-injury and staying on track with God's design for sex. This is a site you can visit frequently to join others in staying inspired to *live free.*

WWW.BREAKAWAYMAG.COM (teen guys) and WWW.BRIOMAG.COM (teen girls)

Both are Focus on the Family ministry sites packed with articles and resources specifically for teens. Includes stories on many topics and issues, but you'll also read about teens who are making a difference.

WWW.CPYU.ORG

The Center for Parent/Youth Understanding is committed to building strong families and offers cutting-edge information and resources on today's youth culture. Founder: Walt Mueller.

WWW.NETADDICTION.COM

This is not a Christian-based site, but the Center for Internet Addiction Recovery is a safe site to find general information on Internet addictions. Director: Dr. Kimberly Young.

Books

Seduced by Sex : Saved by Love—A Journey Out of False Intimacy
False intimacy may have been a part of your online choices, but also your offline lifestyle. If that's true for you, you might want to check out this book. It includes true stories of girls and guys who have struggled through false intimacy and brokenness and later found healing.
Jan Kern, Standard Publishing, 2008

Eyes Wide Open: Avoiding the Heartbreak of Emotional Promiscuity
Even if you've chosen to save sex for marriage, you might still be giving away your heart, one piece at a time. This book starts with the importance of guarding your emotions. One chapter is devoted entirely to setting online boundaries and avoiding the traps of the virtual relationship.
Brienne Murk, Regal Books, 2007

Devotions by Dead People: Secrets of Life from Beyond the Grave
Getting our eyes on life works best when we include spending time with God. This book of fifty devotions reveals how choices made by famous—and infamous!—Bible characters impacted their lives . . . forever.
Lynn Lusby Pratt, Standard Publishing, 2004

Praying from the Gut: An Honest Prayer Journal for Teens
Going deeper in prayer is another way to help balance your online time. This prayer journal encourages you to pray from the head, pray from the heart, and pray from the gut. Be assured: God *is* listening.
Steven James, Standard Publishing, 2004

Be the Wave: Daring to Believe God and Embrace Your Destiny
This book, exploring the stories of ten young men and women from the Bible, will inspire you to step out and be the leader you were meant to be.
Rob Hensser, Standard Publishing, 2005

HOW TO USE THE LIVE FREE BOOKS

Eyes Online : Eyes On Life is from the Live Free series of books. The first two books—*Scars That Wound : Scars That Heal* and *Seduced by Sex : Saved by Love*—deal with self-injury and false intimacy in sexual relationships, respectively. All three Standard Publishing books make great resources for yourself, a friend, or your youth or church group. Here are some ways to use these books:

If you bought any of the books because you are struggling, consider how you might:

- Ask a counselor, pastor, or mentor to work with you through the Going Deeper questions.

- Share the book with a friend you know who might also be struggling.

- Suggest to your youth pastor the idea of starting a small group and working through the stories, questions, and activities together.

If you're seeking to help someone you know who is struggling:

- Read through the tips included in the book and consider specific ways you can encourage your friend.

- Make one of the Live Free books available—without pushing—and let your friend pick it up when they're ready. Maybe include a note offering to listen and encourage.

- Give the book to the pastors at your church and suggest using it as a part of a study or small group.

To use one of the Live Free books as part of a youth program or in a small group:

- Read chapter selections and use the questions at the end of each chapter to kick off an age-appropriate discussion.

- Provide books for those in your youth group who are struggling. Offer regular opportunities to talk through the questions—either one-on-one or in small groups.

- Use the books to help teen/young adult leaders learn how to respond to important issues.

- Keep the books accessible—such as in a church library or pastor's office—for a teen or young adult to pick up and read.

THOUGHTS ON HOLDING A LIVE FREE EVENT

- Plan a one-night, one-day, or weekend event with a focus on practical ways to "live free"—as Jesus talked about in John 8:36.

- In preparing for the event, have some of your youth group members create short videos on the topics you want to discuss.

- Either as a large group or in small groups, use the stories, spiritual applications, and questions from the Live Free books to prompt discussion.

- In small groups, role-play various pressures that young people face; discuss ways that God challenges us to respond.

- Include plenty of time for fun, worship, and prayer.

ALSO FROM THE LIVE FREE SERIES

Scars That Wound : Scars That Heal—A Journey Out of Self-Injury

In this book you walk alongside Jackie, whose arms are marked with reminders of the painful journey she thought she had to take alone. You'll read the true story of God's work in her life, even through her raw struggles and the imperfect responses of others, and the stories of other teens and young adults who have struggled with self-injury.

This book is a finalist for the 2008 ECPA Christian Book of the Year award, Children and Youth category! ISBN: 978-0-7847-2104-9

Seduced by Sex : Saved by Love—A Journey Out of False Intimacy

In the second book in the Live Free series, you'll follow the true story of Suzy, whose search for acceptance and belonging pulled her into the grip of the pressures, lies, and confusion of today's messages about sexuality. You'll read about God's pursuit of Suzy and of others–both guys and girls–who have struggled through false intimacy and brokenness and later found healing. ISBN: 978-0-7847-2158-2

Scars That Wound : Scars That Hea

by Jan Ker

A JOURNEY OUT OF SELF-INJURY // JAN KERN

A LIVE FREE BOOK

SCARS THAT WOUND : SCARS THAT HEAL

2008 ECPA CHRISTIAN BOOK OF THE YEAR FINALIST, CHILDREN & YOUTH

A **LIVE FREE** BOO

"Cutting and other forms of self-injury . . . are cries for redemption and signs of that deep groaning for wholeness and healing. Jan Kern takes readers on a difficult yet necessary journey into understanding self-injury, along with how to enter into that joyous journey that answers the groans."

Walt Mueller, The Center for Parent/Youth Understandir

Find it online at www.standardpub.com,
call 1-800-543-1353, or visit your local Christian bookstore.